A Cotswold
Christmas

2006

to Elaine
from Carol
x.

Advent Market, Cirencester (Photo: *Wilts and Gloucestershire Standard*)

A Cotswold Christmas

JUNE LEWIS-JONES

For my Husband, Ralph, with my love

First published 2006

Tempus Publishing Limited
The Mill, Brimscombe Port,
Stroud, Gloucestershire, GL5 2QG
www.tempus-publishing.com

British Library Cataloguing in Publication Data.
A catalogue record for this book is available from the British Library.

ISBN 0 7524 3975 8

Typesetting and origination by Tempus Publishing Limited
Printed in Great Britain

Contents

Acknowledgements

Firstly, I wish to thank everyone whose work is included in this anthology. The authors and publishers who gave permission to use those writings are acknowledged, as appropriate, with the relevant pieces. Inevitably, as with the case of some features that appeared in publications that are no longer extant, it has proved impossible to trace the current copyright holders. I can only apologise for such omissions.

In particular, for their exceptional effort in getting their contributions to me, despite having to meet demanding deadlines in their own busy schedule, I accord special appreciation for their interest and support to: Pam Ayres; The Rt Revd Michael Perham, The Bishop of Gloucester; Michael Boyes; Johnny Coppin; Diane Harris; Meg Harrison, Everyman Theatre; Katie Jarvis; Robert Johnston, Bibury Court; Chloe Lees; Mike Lowe, Editor, *Cotswold Life*; John Shakles, Chairman of The John Moore Society; Elizabeth Speller; Skip Walker, Editor, *Wilts and Gloucestershire Standard*.

Photographic credits are given with the relevant pictures; all other illustrations are my own.

INTRODUCTION

What a pleasure it has been to compile this anthology, A Cotswold Christmas, for Christmas is such a special time: a benchmark in our calendar, a touchstone of our senses; the word alone so evocative of a myriad of images – a virtual kaleidoscope of sights and sounds and smells that weave a unique magic that transcends all ages and time. Set these elements in the special area of the Cotswolds and you have a heady brew as intoxicating as Charles Dickens's homemade Christmas punch.

The Cotswolds are steeped in history and hoary tradition, and a natural beauty of such simple charm as breeds its own culture that have inspired writers throughout the ages, from Chaucer to Laurie Lee. So, selecting from the rich store of their writings has not been an easy task, but my aim was to build up a story of Christmas from diverse sources – reflecting the diversity of Cotswold characters and characteristics across a couple of centuries of social change, punctuated with a handful of pieces from the literary greats.

We have been tenacious to our traditions such as the ancient rituals of mumming, Morris dancing and wassailing and these can still be found enacted in some corner or other of the Cotswolds. Advent markets have been a fairly recent community event in the Christmastide calendar and set the scene for the fairly frenetic flurry of school nativity plays, carol services, church bazaars and festive fairs leading up to the big day itself. Just how Christmas has been celebrated under differing circumstances has been gleaned from diaries and journals from Charles Dickens's family to those of a village church rector and a chapel minister to the modern-day monks of Prinknash; from the chronicles of a Cotswold country squire to the austere audit of Victorian workhouses, and from recollections collected of Stroud Maternity Hospital at Christmas to a ten-year-old's letter to Santa – and even the thoughts of Father and Mother Christmas whose daughter was born on Christmas Day!

A look at the festive board over the last century, from an intimate dinner party devised by Mrs Beeton in Edwardian times to the calculations for providing 400 dinners in the war-torn forties, and as many hungry children from the school kitchen in the seventies, shows just how much and how little change there has been in the traditional plum pudding – the centrepiece of all Christmas dinners.

Storytelling has been our oral heritage since man developed a communal language – and it is at Christmastide that it comes down through the ages, telling and retelling the story of Christmas itself in the familiar lines of the age-old carols; tales of long ago – of ghostly goings-on and legends and folklore take on their own mystical moment at the Yuletide fireside. And we can boast one of the best-loved folk of fable, whose life story began as true fact when Dick Whittington developed from his Cotswold home roots to become the folk hero of pantomime.

Finally, the Christmas card picture of Christmas is of a familiar scene, the church or street, a field or cottage under a blanket of snow – transforming an everyday place to a winter wonderland. The reality is that very few of us have experienced a truly white Christmas, of which we all secretly dream. The weather is a constant topic of conversation and concern throughout all seasons, but takes on a new dimension at Christmastide, so as this collection of writings slides into the New Year, it is interesting to look back to those that have gone before and end with those winters of yesteryear.

And, of course, Christmas is a time for wishes – so, may I wish all who read this book all that you would wish for you and yours at this Christmastide.

June Lewis-Jones

Advent

My Cotswold Valley

By Laurie Lee

Laurie Lee reminisced about his childhood in the Slad Valley, that he immortalised in his country classic, Cider with Rosie, *for* My Cotswold Life *series, published by* Cotswold Life *in 1995. Laurie was interviewed by June Lewis in his favourite village pub, The Woolpack at Slad, and the article is reproduced here by permission of the publishers of* Cotswold Life *magazine.*

My Cotswold life began as a three-year-old child awakening to the sounds and sights and smells of this lovely Slad Valley. It was a secret world which belongs only to childhood, when my senses absorbed the wonder of wildlife and plants around me. As a two-and-a-half feet toddler you lead a kind of pigmy life; you can go where grown ups cannot go. You are allowed to pass freely among the insects and animals, you are down among the butterfly chrysalis and the dank roots and tangled grasses. You know where to find the red soldier and the blue chalk butterflies, the badger trails and the marks of vole, the stoat and shrew. I was most sharply in focus with the natural details of this valley from the birdsong to the local dialect, the poetry of the words passed from neighbour to neighbour over the garden fence. When I was a child I thought the whole world was like Slad; my whole existence centred around the village and its valley. Here, in this isolated rural life we were able to be both saints and savages: as a church choirboy I was a saint – or at least I thought so – I revelled in the rich language of the James I bible and sang the hymns as lustily as anyone; in the woods we became

Laurie Lee with June Lewis-Jones in his favourite pub, The Woolpack at Slad

savages – not to draw blood, just simply living a joyous life with nature through the passing seasons.

I did not see Tetbury until I was 17, and I thought Tewkesbury was somewhere in Poland. I was a young man when I left this valley; at 19. I waved it farewell to see the world. I have seen the world now. My travels have taken me throughout Europe, Asia, Scandinavia, the Americas, the Middle East and the Far East, but like the homing birds which return year after year from their wintering in warmer climates, I have returned. Nowhere in the world have I seen anything to replace this special place, this Cotswold narrow valley.

A GLOUCESTERSHIRE YEOMAN'S HOUSE IN THE EIGHTEENTH CENTURY

By J.B. Partridge

This extract of an inventory taken of the farm effects of Abraham Shipton, considered to be a well-to-do Cotswold yeoman, was discovered among the County Archives and featured in an article by J.B. Partridge in the April 1938 issue of The Gloucestershire Countryside *magazine which is now extinct, therefore no copyright holder can be traced. Although not strictly relevant to Christmastide, it gives us a fascinating glimpse into the daily life of a Cotswold household in 1743.*

Abraham Shipton died in 1743 at his home in Nailsworth, then a chapelry of the parish of Horsley (the house with its outbuildings, built somewhere about the time of the Spanish Armada, formed a group of four dwellings known as Barn Close in 1938). Abraham was hardly laid to rest before an inventory of his goods and chattels was taken for probate.

The best dinner service comprised 11 dishes, 1 dozen plates and 1 cheese plate in pewter; for everyday use there were 13 trenchers, valued at 4d the lot. The big table-board and two 'joynt-stools' were worth 7s in all, two lesser table-boards, 'ashen and 'helm' chairs, a salt-box and a candle-box were in the kitchen. In the hearth were fire-irons, hangalls, twy-crook (like a big letter 'S' for hanging pots on) a jack and three spits for roasting and various pots and pans – all valued by weight: iron 7d per pound, brass 8d, and pewter 6d. The brewhouse and 'seller' contained various tubs and barrels.

The whole village turned out to welcome Mr Gardner Bazley and his bride home to Hatherop Castle after their wedding in 1902

In the parlour was a 'bucking basket' worth 8d, no doubt like the one in which Falstaff was conveyed away by the Merry Wives. All the men's thick smocks, dirty from field and stable, all the hand-spun and hand-woven linen sheets (ten of Abraham's were worth 2s apiece), all the coarse aprons and body linen, went to the 'buck-washing' – a word lost to us now, though Randwick has a proverb: 'It's like Runnick's bucking, it'll look better when it's dry'.

The only furniture of note in the parlour was a clock 'and clock-case' valued at £1 5s. The total worth of the day house, meaning dairy, ('deye' was once used as the name for the female servant who cared for milk and poultry) with its churns, cheese press, 'trendles' (wooden tubs) was £1 14s 6d. Salting down of meat for winter usually took place in November: in the pantry was a 'powdering tub' for pickling beef; a side and a half of bacon were on the kitchen rack; 32 cheeses, worth £1 were in the cheese-loft, butter salted down and 'rendered' lard.

Above all, the barn and cornloft held 32 bushels of wheat, valued at £3 10s, 15 bushels of threshed barley £1, and one stack of barley 'in the straw' £3 – no doubt to be carried to the mill that lay close at hand down by the water. Little livestock was left (no doubt some had already been killed off for salting down for winter). All that was left were 3 cows, worth £12 and one mare £2 10s; there was a 'pig's trow' in the court, but no pigs in the sty. The biggest single item in the whole of the Inventory was one Hay Mow valued at £7 10s.

Among the stack of homely linen we read of one newfangled set of calico pillow-slips, 5 Dowlas pillow-drawers made in France – these with pepper bought for the funeral were the only foreign things in the house.

The total value of Abraham Shipton's goods and chattels were appraised at a total of £64 16s 9d, after the parson and clerk had had their dues; £4 13s 4d spent on '40 days to the Poor; 6d for laying Father out' and '6d for shaveing Father' had been paid by his daughter Hannah as executor.

BOAR'S HEAD CAROL

From Queen's College, Oxford

Reproduced from information generously supplied by the Keeper of the Archives at Queen's College, Oxford University.

The ancient ceremony of bringing in a boar's head is carried out on a weekday in the week before Christmas at Queen's College, commemorating the university student, Copcot, who was attacked by a wild boar in the woods around Oxford while studying Aristotle. With only a book in his hand to defend himself against the creature,

Copcot thrust it down the boar's throat, exclaiming *Graecum est* (Greek), and the boar expired. As the focal point of the festive dinner, a boar's head, wreathed in holly, bay and rosemary, with an orange in its mouth, is borne in with great pomp and ceremony on a silver platter accompanied by the college choristers singing the Boar's Head carol. When the dish is placed on the high table, the provost presents the chief chorister with the orange, and distributes sprigs of the holly, bay and rosemary that had decorated the boar's head among the guests.

The words of the carol are translated as:

> The Boar's Head in hand bear I,
> Bedecked with bays and rosemary,
> And I pray you, my masters, be merry.
> Quot estis in convivio (You who are at the banquet)

> The Boar's Head as I understand,
> Is the rarest dish in all this land,
> Which thus bedecked with a gay garland
> Let us servire cantico.

A COTSWOLD VILLAGE
CHRISTMAS REJOICINGS

By J. Arthur Gibbs

Joseph Arthur Gibbs, to give the author his full name, chronicled the life and times of the small hamlet of Ablington, the neighbouring village of Bibury and the Coln Valley within the wider compass of the social and economic structure as the long Victorian era was ending. This evergreen classic, A Cotswold Village, from which the following extract is taken, has never been out of print since the author's untimely death in 1899, barely a year after his book was originally published by John Murray. As a young squire of Ablington Manor, with Eton and Oxford as an educational background, Gibbs drew on a number of literary sources to give emphasis to much of his thoughts, but his deep interest in the Cotswold countryside and its characters are the bedrock on which the book has come to be valued. One of the tributes paid to Arthur Gibbs when he died suddenly at the early age of thirty-one was in a letter from one of the villagers stating, 'He went in and out as a friend among us'. It is the simple recording of how Christmas was celebrated in his small pocket of the Coln Valley over a century ago that draws such an evocative picture of the true spirit of Christmastide.

Chedworth Band playing carols at Bibury Court, Christmas 2005, just down the road from J. Arthur Gibbs's home at Ablington Manor, from where he wrote of the Chedworth Band playing over 100 years ago

Listen to the Christmas bells ringing two miles away at Barnsley village!
I can never tire of the sound here, for it is only on very still days that it
reaches us across the wolds.

> Hark! In the air, around, above
> The Angelic Muse soars and swells,
> And in the Garden that I love
> I hear the sound of Christmas bells.
> Alfred Austin

I have culled these lines from the poet laureate's charming 'Christmas
Carol', as they are both singularly beautiful and singularly appropriate
to our Cotswold village.

I take the liberty of saying that in our little hamlet there *is* peace and
goodwill 'twixt rich and poor at Christmas-time.

> Now is the ancient feud forgot,
> The growing grudge is laid aside.

Our humble rejoicings during this last Christmas were very similar to
those of 100 years ago. They included a grand smoking concert at the
club, during which the Mummers gave an admirable performance of
their old play, then a big feed for every man, woman and child in the
manor house; added to which we received visits from carol singers and
musicians of all kinds to the number of seventy-two, reckoning up the
total aggregate of the different bands, all of whom were welcomed, for
Christmas comes but once a year, after all, and 'the more the merrier'
should be our motto at this time. So from villages three and four miles
away came bands of children to sing the old, old songs. The brass band,
including old grey-haired men who fifty years ago with strings and
woodwind led the psalmody at Chedworth Church, come too, and
play inside the hall. We do not brew at home nowadays. Even such
old-fashioned Conservatives as old Mr Peregrine, senior, have at length
given up the custom, so we cannot, like Sir Roger, allow a greater
quantity of malt to our small beer at Christmas; but we take good care

to order in some four or five eighteen-gallon casks at this time. Let it be
added that we never saw any man the worse for drink in consequence
of this apparent indiscretion. But then, we have a butler of the old
school.

When we held our Yuletide revels in the manor house, and the
old walls rang with laughter and merriment of the whole hamlet
(for farmers as well as labourers honoured us), it occurred to me
that the bigotphones, which had been lying by in a cupboard for
about a twelvemonth, might amuse the company. Bigotphones, I must
explain to those readers who are uninitiated, are delightfully simple
contrivances fitted with reed mouthpieces – exact representations in
mockery of the various instruments that make up a brass band – but
composed of strong cardboard, and dependent solely on the judicious
application of the human lips and the skilful modulation of the human
voice for their effect. These being produced, an impromptu band
was formed; young Peregrine seized the bassoon, the carter took the
clarinet, the shepherd the French horn, the cowman the trombone,
and, seated at the piano, I myself conducted the orchestra. Never
before have I been so astonished as I was by the unexpected musical
ability displayed. No matter what tune I struck up, that heterogeneous
orchestra played it as if they had been doing nothing else all their
lives. *The British Grenadiers, The Eton Boating Song, Two Lovely Black
Eyes* (solo, young Peregrine on the bassoon), *A Fine Hunting Day*
– all and sundry were performed in perfect time and without a
false note. Singularly enough, it is very difficult for the voice to
'go flat' on the bigotphone. Then, not content with these popular
songs we inaugurated a dance. Now could be seen the beautiful and
accomplished Miss Peregrine doing the light fantastic round the
stone floor of the hall to the tune of 'See me dance the polka'; then,
too, the stately Mrs Peregrine insisted on our playing 'Sir Roger de
Coverley', and it was danced with such pomp and ceremony which
such occasions alone are wont to show. None of your 'kitchen lancers'
for us hamlet folk; we leave that kind of thing to the swells and nobs.
Tom Peregrine alone was baffled. Whilst his family in general were
bowing there, curtseying here, clapping hands and 'passing under to

the right' in the usual 'Sir Roger' style, he stood in grey homespun of the best material (I never yet saw a Cotswold man in a vulgar chessboard suit), and as he stood he marvelled greatly, exclaiming now and then, 'Well, I never; this is something new to be sure!' 'I never saw such things in all my life, never!' He would not dance; but, seizing one of the bigotphones, he blew into it until I was in some anxiety lest he should have an apoplectic fit. I need scarcely say he failed to produce a single note.

Thus our Yuletide festivities passed away, all enjoying themselves immensely, and thus was sealed the bond of fellowship and of goodwill 'twixt class and class for the coming year.

Whilst the younger folks danced, the fathers of the hamlet walked on tiptoe with fearful tread around the house, looking at the faded family portraits. I was pleased to find that what they liked best was the ancient armour; for said they, 'Doubtless squire wore that in the old battles hereabouts, when Oliver Cromwell was round these parts.' I pointed out the picture of the man who built the house 300 years ago, they surrounded it, and gazed at the features for a great length of time; indeed, I feared that they would never come away, so fascinated were they by this relic of antiquity, illustrating the ancient though simple annals of their village.

I persuaded the head of our Mummers troop to write down their play as it was handed down to him by his predecessors. This he did in a fine bold hand on four sides of foolscap. Unfortunately the literary quality of the lines is so poor that they are hardly worth reproducing, except as a specimen of the poetry of very early times handed down by oral tradition. Suffice it to say that the *dramatis personae* are five in number – viz, Father Christmas, St George, a Turkish knight, the doctor and an old woman. All are dressed in paper flimsies of various shapes and colours. First of all enters Father Christmas.

In comes I old Father Christmas,
Welcome in or welcome not,
Sometimes cold and sometimes hot,
I hope Father Christmas will never be forgot.

Then St George comes in, and after a great deal of bragging he fights the 'most dreadful battle that ever was known,' his adversary being the knight 'just come from Turkey-land,' with the inevitable result that the Turkish knight falls. This brings in the doctor, who suggests the following remedies:

> Give him a bucket of hot ashes to eat,
> Groom him down with a besom stick,
> And give him a yard and a half of pump water to drink.

For these offices he mentions that his fee is fifty guineas, but he will take ten pounds, adding:

> I can cure the itchy pitchy,
> Palsy and the gout;
> Pains within or pains without;
> A broken leg or a broken arm,
> Or a broken limb of any sort.
> I cured old Mother Roundabout.

He declares that he is not one of those 'quack doctors who go about from house to house telling you more lies in one half-hour than what you can find true in seven years.'

So the knight just come from Turkey-land is resuscitated and sent back to his own country.

Last of all, the old woman speaks:

> In comes I old Betsy Bub;
> On my shoulder I carry my tub,
> And in my hand a dripping-pan
> Don't you think I'm a jolly old man.

The Mummers' play, of which the above is a very brief resume, lasts about half an hour, and includes many songs of a topical nature.

Yes, Christmas is Christmas still in the heart of old England. We are apt to talk of the good old days that are no more, lamenting the customs and country sports that have passed away, but not let us forget that 200 years hence, when we who are living now will have long passed 'that bourne from which no traveller returns,' our descendents, as they sit round their hearths at Yule-tide, may in the same way regret the grand old times when Victoria – the greatest monarch of all ages – was Queen of England. 200 years hence, I say, the Victorian era – time of blessed peace and unexampled prosperity – will be pronounced by all unprejudiced judges as the true days of merrie England. Let us, then, though not unmindful of the past, pin our faith firmly on the present and the future, *Carpe diem* should be our motto in these fleeting times, and, above all, progress, not retrogression. Let us, as the old, old sound of the village bells comes to us over the rolling downs this New Year's eve, recall to mind

… the primal sympathy
Which having been must ever be.

Mumming

By June Lewis-Jones

Man's life has always been a fight against some sort of odds: primitive man struggled for mere survival and existence, and our forefathers fought against poverty and ignorance, but the facility they possessed for creating some vestige of magic and wonder round the simple complexities of sheer living seem to be lost to us. Perhaps we, in this sophisticated age of technology, are more educated than our ancestors, but are we as wise? Once we lose the desire to make our own amusement, to participate in the rich pageantry of custom, or cease to entertain tradition when it raises its hoary head, we sever those ancient ties which have stretched across the centuries to leaven the lot of living and bring just that little aura of magic which we all need.

The origin of Mumming is rooted in antiquity. That it was a pre-Christian fertility rite is determined by the death and resurrection theme which is the nucleus of all Mumming plays. In fact, play seems a rather grandiose description of what is, in short, a ritual practised by local folk fearfully transformed at Christmastide to become the luck-bringers, the harbingers of hope for the earth to spring to life again after the old year has died. The Mummers, therefore, were held in a certain awe; He-next-door and Old-Thingamebob-from-t'other-end all the year they may be, but emerging from the winter's dark night, disguised in anything that came to hand, imbued with their intent and whatever hospitality they were afforded along the way, they weaved their weird and magical thread into the fabric of the festive season.

Extremely popular in Tudor times, the masques and mimicry expanded into what we now know as Mumming. Partly from superstition, partly from illiteracy, and in no small part due to the faith that someone would always take part, the plays were never written down. Preserved by tenacious memory, the strength of the Mumming play depended entirely on its purely oral tradition. This, in turn, bred truly regional versions, rich in the dialect of the county; the rustic humour sharpened by reference to local characteristics. Allowed this artistic licence, and spending a great deal of time studying in depth the complex subject of folklore, both in personal research and consultation with the leading authorities in ritual drama, I wrote a version for Fairford in 1974, using scraps and fragments of half-remembered lines that were still in the memories of local residents from what they had seen and heard before the First World War – a benchmark for the end of the English Mummers, as so many of the characters fought for real in real uniform, taking and losing their centuries-old traditional lines in the trenches.

Fairford Mummers reviving the age-old tradition in 1976 (Photo: *Wiltshire Newspaper*)

The Fairford Mumming play is based on the essential fight between right and evil: Robin Hood represents a kind of universally accepted god-hero of all time; his adversary is Belzebub, whom I based on the scaly old devil in St Mary's church famous west window. I telescoped the roles of Master of Ceremonies, Lord of Misrule and old Father Christmas into a spirit of Christmas. Johnny Dout is a motley of clown, fool and doctor's assistant: Dout (Do out) refers to the sweeping out of the old year's ashes and indicating the area in which the action takes place – the symbolic magic circle. Worried Jack carries life's troubles on his back, giving a Humpty Dumpty kind of appearance of morose character.

Doctor-do-no-good, a farcical character whose primitive functions have been analogised from Greek comedy to the mountebanks of the Renaissance, miraculously resurrects the dead man (the departed year brought magically to life in the spring).

An Oxford professor once asked why women were traditionally excluded, making it a purely masculine ritual. The old Mummer replied, 'It ain't for the likes of 'oomanfolk, Mumming be more like parson's work!'

So, one break with tradition as our cast always included women for the decade we made Mumming part of our local Christmastide until nearby Kempsford unearthed a Victorian version and revived it, taking over where we left off. And, of course, it is all illegal!

Mummery comes under the terms of masques, which along with 'revelling, epicurisme, dancing, drinking, stage plaies and carnale pomp and jollity' were banned by the Puritans and the law was never taken off the Statute Book. But the law also states that a Christmas dinner must not exceed three courses, men cannot be shaved or have a hair cut on Christmas Day, when sport is curtailed to practising archery – although one can 'vault' or 'leap' with impunity! An Act of 1551 states that folk should walk to church; any carriage found near the church can be confiscated, and not attending at least one service on Christmas Day carries a fine of 1s. None of these laws seem to have been repealed – meanwhile Mumming and making merry is still carried on by traditional bands at Marshfield and Gloucester and a few revivals in odd corners of the Cotswolds.

Fairford Mumming Play

Spirit of Christmas: [knocks on the door begging leave for the Mummers to be admitted] Will ee let the Mummers in?
(When admitted, the entire characters file in, led by Spirit of Christmas, with waits or Morris dancers or any musicians bringing up the rear. Each character acknowledges the audience with a greeting, waving streamers and ringing bells as they progress in a big circle to indicate the 'playing area' needed. Then exit.)

Christmas: [enters ringing handbell]
Afore the rest, Yere comes I
Let not the Spirit of Christmas pass ee by
Thee's opened the door and let us in
So we hopes your favours us'll win

Johnny: [rushes in sweeping a circle with broom]
Room, room, for me and my broom
I'll swip away until there's room
Room, room, give us room to rhyme
Our Mummers' Play this Christmastime

Christmas:
Come in now, Robin Hood
Show us why thou bist so good

Robin: [swaggering in and brandishing a sword, announces himself]
Robin, Bold Robin, from those days of yore

Like all the brave knights that's gone afore
I defend the right and help the poor

Johnny: [creeps up to Robin and looks at him in awe]
What? Just like Saint Jarge in days of old
Bist thee like ee – bist thee as bold?
[advances with broom]

Robin: [swirls his sword and Johnny jumps back to hide behind Christmas]
Dragons, bah! As bold and bolder
'Cos I'm that much older
Universal Nature God hero, me
Come yere to Fairford for all to see

Christmas:
Ee's right enow, for this yere fight
Represents evil a-fighting right *[rubs beard thoughtfully]*
Well, same difference somewhere, for right
Is right: I reckon on that's right
I knew I'd chew off more than I could bite
By agreeing to take this yere part tonight
Any ways there's about to be a fight

Johnny: [excited]
A fight? Tonight? Oh, my goodnight! *[sweeping energetically]*
Room, room, for me and my broom
If it's going to be now, 'twill be sooner than soon

Belzebub: [leaps in, banging pan with a club and brandishing the club at the audience]
In comes I, old Belzebub
In my hand I carries a club
In 'tother hand a dripping pan
To make mincemeat out o' that righteous man

Johnny: [creeping up to Belzebub with mock bravado]
  How now, thou little fellow
  Thy talk is very bold
  Hasn't yeard of Robin 'ere
  An' all they knights of old?

Belzebub: [glowering at Johnny and advancing on him menacingly with club raised: Johnny dodges him]
  Who bist thee, as can't be hit
  With thy gurt yud and little wit?

Johnny:
  If thee that is so big and stout
  Thee and I'll have a bout *[Johnny and Belzebub spar with broom and club]*

Christmas: [steps in, reprimanding Johnny]
  With a yud so big and a wit so small
  Thou should'st endeavour to please us all

Robin: [coming forward and brandishing sword]
  This Belzebub in guise tonight
  Is really spoiling for a fight
  Well yere I be to maintain all right
  If I were King George, he'd be a Turkish knight

Christmas:
  An' if thou was't Saint Jarge – he a dragonly knight

Johnny:
  Or Arthur Abland, the Tanner by right

[Belzebub and Robin fence with their weapons – very mechanical movements, like a slow dance. Each following bit of dialogue ending with a clash of weapons to give it emphasis]

Robin:
  Tanner *[clash]* or dragon *[clash]* or ancient Turk *[clash]*
  From battle with any, I'll not shirk *[clash]*

Belzebub:
  Let's see just how hard thee bist hardy *[clash]*
  Afore I flattens thee into a Fairford lardy *[clash]*

Christmas:
  So, it's lard ee 'as in his dripping pan *[clash]*

Belzebub:
  Aarh! Ain't I just a jolly ol' man *[clash]*

[Johnny gets closer to the fighting pair so Belzebub turns his attention to Johnny, who jumps astride his broom]

Belzebub
  'Cos if I wusser than bad
  I'd have thee as a skimmerlad

Johnny: [trembling]
  On top o' pot? I reckon 'ee 'ood

Christmas: [amused – and explains to audience]
  The Cotsall's answer to a Yorkshire pud!

Belzebub: [menaces Christmas]
  An' what if I gives thee a clump

Christmas: [protecting his hat]
  Ay – just ee mind me feggy dump

Robin: [defending Johnny and Christmas]
  Dust talk on 'er and she allus as 'ee?

Belzebub: [riding Robin's sword thrust with a disdainful flip of his pan]
  'Er and she is allus 'ee *[reflects for a moment, rubs his chin then laughs]*
  'Except for tomcats and our Mother Country
    They together be allus she

Robin:
  I'll hit ee into middle of next week *[clash]*

Belzebub: [mockingly, turns to audience]
Says sommat dunnee every time 'ee do speak *[taken off guard, Belzebub falls from a blow from Robin]*

Robin: [kneels down and appeals to audience]
  He's died a death, and bleeds with blood;
  Go and get Doctor Do-no-good

Christmas: [calls]
  Doctor!

Doctor: [walks in]
  Well, I'd sooner kill than cure
  So what dust really want I for?

Christmas:
  Afore us offers thee a fee
  Us wants to know a bit about thee
  [pointing to the others] Dust come from same parts as I, thee and he?

Doctor:
  Well, I don't come from where
  They knits hoss shoes

Christmas: [curiously]
  Or thatch thy pigsties with pancakes?

Johnny:
  And have beef steak stiles in Plum Pudding Lane?

Robin:
  Or give thy hoss 'ot ashes to drink?

Doctor: [shuddering]
  Of wusser fates I could not think
  I comes from where they reads their Bible off the glass
  And the old Fairford Flier flies no more, alas!
  But 'tother flies twice as fast as sound

Christmas:
  They'll meet themselves a-coming back, I'll be bound
  [Christmas, Robin and Johnny nod to each other, satisfied with the Doctor's credentials]

Robin:
   Then of thy cures, Doctor, thou canst now speak

Doctor:
  Well, there was Eliza died middle of next week
  The sleeping sickness kept her awake

Johnny: [running round, very excited]
  Room, room, for me and my broom
  [importantly] I can cure a magpie with the stitch
  [chuckling] Cut off 'is yud and throw it in the ditch

Doctor: [questioning Johnny]
  But what of the itch – the palsy and the gout
  Pains within and pains without?
  Then there's the whatsit
  You gets in your wheresit
  Just like old whoseit …

Christmas:
Who?

Johnny:
Had?

Robin:
What?

Doctor:
Old who-je-ma-flip
From where-ja-ma-call it
Had the thing-a-me jig
In his back-a-beyond
But with a tiddly-push
And a hows-your-father
'Twas Bobs-your-uncle
And 'tis if it's not
I allus remembered
What I never forgot

Christmas:
But canst thee cure this dead man who's died?

Johnny: [boasting]
I could a-done it afore I even tried

Robin:
Stop thy argyfying Johnny Dout, thee bist a clown

Johnny:
Master John Dout to thee – I've a bit of renown

Doctor: [examining Belzebub by the light of a candle]
Now if he'd rheumatiz in all four elbows on his knee

I'd have to charge just twice my normal fee
The bellows, please, Master Dout
[blows into Belzebub's face] There, there, Belzebub, now thee's fit to shout
[as Belzebub rises, Johnny chatters excitedly]

Johnny:
  All is well, Bubzly Bell

[All characters ring a bell, Johnny gives Belzebub the candle, which he puts in his frying pan and the Doctor presents him with a Book of Fees]

Belzebub: *[slinking away]*
  The Book, the candle, and the bell
  Signals my return to … oh, well! *[exits to the ringing of bells]*

Jack: *[entering with a doleful expression]*
  Here comes I old Worried Jack
  With all me troubles on me back
  My hide is thick and broad's me back
  Redundant now – can't get the sack
  I pays so much insurance, can't enjoy being ill

Doctor: *[offering a huge pill]*
  And thee can't afford sugar to sweeten the pill

Jack: *[still harping on his misfortunes and turning to the Doctor for treatment]*
  Last Christmas Day I turned the spit
  I burnt my fingers and felt it hit
  The spark jumped on and off the table
  And the frying pan beat the ladle

Belzebub: *[creeps in with a dragon's mask on and taunts Jack]*
  Thee bist an old Worrit, I can see

What's do then if thee was like me
Since they thought about Mumming their plans for I
Were to get rid of I quick, so dyud I must die

Jack:
But thee allus comes back in some sort of guise

Belzebub:
Ann thee hast all the complaints of which no-one dies
*[A short fight breaks out between Jack and Belzebub, Robin joins in, now
with a cloak and St George headgear on and steps in to take over the fight
– again, slow and mechanical movements. Christmas raises his staff and calls
a halt to the fighting. Jack examines his wounds, the Doctor busies himself
with his bag and Johnny runs round sweeping a circle clear again]*

Johnny:
Room, room, for me and my broom *[turns to Belzebub and points to
the cleared space on the floor]*
There's room for thee to die, dyud again *[as Belzebub is taken off guard
again, Robin triumphantly finishes him off. Belzebub curls up this time,
hanging his head in dejection]*

Christmas: [holding up Robin's hand]
And right is right
Well, that's quite plain
[calls to Doctor] Come yere, Doc – live up to thy name

Johnny: [doubting the Doctor's ability, offers a word of advice]
If 'ee woke up dyud
That wouldn't be natural for she *[rubbing his hands together gleefully
at his joke]*
That 'ud be worth only 'alf your normal fee

Rest Together:
But, Doctor, thou must try

Doctor: [*with dignity*]
Don't thee thou I [*opens his bag and offers Blezebub medicine out of a long spoon*]

Belzebub: [*rising slowly and giving the Doctor a grateful leer*]
Thee's done did it
And 'tis as was [turning to the rest, menaces them in turn, leaving Robin until last]

Christmas: [*intervening*]
Hold hands, and let thy quarrels fall
Thee'll beat thy bones all to a meat

Doctor:
And get no 'quaintance at all

Robin:
Remember us poor Mummers who strive

Belzebub:
To keep Merry England's traditions alive

Christmas:
So we wish you a Merry Christmas

All:
And peace on earth, Wassail, Wassail

Johnny: [*running round with his broom as the collectors go round*]
Room, room, for me and my broom
'Twill be Christmas Day very soon

All: [*as departing to the ringing of bells, they jig in unison to exit*]
We wish you a Merry Christmas
We wish you a Merry Christmas

Waterley Bottom Mummers at Dursley, 1972

Doctor: [*bringing up the rear – adds meaningly*]
And a healthy New Year

FROM THE NOTEBOOKS OF A
GLOUCESTERSHIRE CURATE

By R.H. Penley

The following summary of the biographical notes and extracts from the notebooks of Kingscote Daunt, who was curate of Owlpen in the eighteenth century, are taken from R.H. Penley's article in Gloucestershire Countryside, *April and October 1935 issues respectively. The entries relating to Christmastide expenses give a brief insight into the economic and social conditions of the 1700s, and give a different impression of the culture and position of the unbeneficed clergy in the reign of George II from that derived from a number of the historical and fictional writings of the day.*

Kingscote Daunt was born in 1723, the youngest son of Thomas Daunt whose family had been established at Owlpen since the late fifteenth century, when John Daunt married Margery Owlpen, the daughter and sole heiress of Robert Owlpen – the last of that name to hold the manor of Owlpen. Kingscote Daunt was sent up to Oxford in 1740 and entered Pembroke College. In 1745 he was ordained deacon in Gloucester Cathedral, obtained his MA in 1747 and ordained priest in 1748; his licence was endorsed to enable him to serve the church of Owlpen, where he made his home at the Manor House. Soon after becoming curate of Owlpen he received rent from a small estate in County Cork and was thus able to lend his father money. Kingscote valued his books at £40, which may be compared with his stipend of £10 as curate, not paid at all punctually by Mr Warneford, the Rector.

Kingscote Daunt commenced as curate of Owlpen in December 1748 and the following accounts (original spelling has been retained) relate to the expenses he paid out at Christmas 1748.

Paid Thomas Pierce for Shooing	0 2 6
Gave the Maid at Christmas	1 0
Gave Tyndale the Fiddler at twice	2 0
Laid out with the Scotchman	1 8 6
Gave Doctor Perry for advice	10 6
Paid out of my Christmas Rent, 1748	
Paid William	11 0
Paid for exchanging bill	3 10
Paid to Clarke and spent at Dursley	4 3
Paid my Brother	2 4 0
Paid my Mother	14 0
Paid Mr Colborne the Apothecary	2 7 0
Paid for Mr Ledwel's cheese	1 6 0
Laid out with the Pedlar	1 11 6
Gave the Physician	10 6
Paid for several things	5 6
Paid for Oats to my Brother	8 0
Paid for two pair of Shoos	10 0
Paid a quarters Shaving	4 6
Paid Roger Lord the Taylor	1 18 0
Paid John Fereby for making my breeches	7 6
Paid for making three Shirts	6 0
Paid Mr Scott for a brown wigg	1 1 0
Paid for a qr of Tobacco	6
Paid for a Saddle cloth, &c	2 10 0
Paid Mr Huntridge the Surgeon	1 1 0
Pd Gabriel Barns for wine	1 1 0
Spent at Tetbury at twice & at Wotton	10 0
Paid Mr Vines for Rum	10 0

Paid to Mr Wightwick for Potter the Barber	1 1 0
I have money remaining:-	
One three pound twelve	3 12 0
10 pieces at 1: 16: 0 each	18 0 0
4 Guineas	4 4 0

Advertisements for the 'most rare invention' of the new mail coach which
'flew' across the Cotswolds, along with the carriages, post chaises and carriers'
carts in the eighteenth century (from cover of *Gloucestershire Countryside*)

Old Gosditch Street, Cirencester – from an engraving of 1804

Vicars' Notes from the 'East Cotswold Church Monthly', December 1968

Extracts from vicars' letters to their parishioners as published in the regional magazine, December 1968 issue

ALDSWORTH

My dear Parishioners

You will be glad to know that the Christmas Festival this year will be marked by the use, for the first time, of a lovely new white and gold Altar Frontal, which a friend of ours, who is very clever at all kinds of embroidery, has very kindly worked, and which we are glad to give for the use of the Church. I hope to dedicate this gift at the Midnight Service on Christmas Eve, and we hope that it may be admired by you all. May I remind you that for next year the subscription for this Church Monthly magazine is 7/- for the year. There are still several amounts outstanding for this year, which should be paid as soon as possible.

Your sincere friend and Vicar, Eric G. Pritchard

COLESBOURNE AND RENDCOMB

My dear Friends

I hope the Christmas Day Services will be convenient for the majority of people. With Summer Time in the winter I thought a Holy

Christmas Day gifts certificate of the First World War

Communion Service at 9 am would be early enough and dark enough to begin the day this year.

If you wish to help in the work of the Church of England Children's Society which cares for 5,000 unwanted and homeless children, please put your gift in the envelope provided. Some families like to make a special collection at their Christmas Dinner for orphans and Miss Thorn can provide collecting boxes if you would like one in your home.

Wishing you a very Happy Christmas.

Sydney T. Lambert, Rector

CHEDWORTH WITH YANWORTH AND STOWELL

Dear Friends

We look forward to Christmas. It is a joyful season when we hear again with the shepherds of old the heavenly message; but there is not peace on earth and millions of people hardly have the bare necessities of life. But this does not invalidate the message. It was just to such a world Jesus came and still comes. He Himself was born in an enemy occupied country, away from home in what was no doubt a rather dirty and draughty stable. Though the intervening years have given that birthplace a romantic glow, it could not have been much fun at the time, and was most humiliating for Joseph and Mary and the Child. Jesus had such a humble birth that there might be no one, however poor, who could not look to him with hope. To help you make the best of Christmas I have given you a full range of services to choose from.

Yours sincerely, Arthur Dodds

Carol Services included one at the Seven Tuns public house in Chedworth, and church collections for the month of October from Yanworth and Stowell ranged from £1 19s in the first week to 2s 3d in the last week.

COLN ST ALDWYNS WITH HATHEROP AND QUENINGTON

One of our main regrets this month must be the retirement of Miss Brindle from our Church of England School at Hatherop, who has been at the school for 34 years and has lovingly shepherded successive generations of children through the junior stage. The whole community owes her an immense debt of gratitude.

For several years there has been a most attractive Crib at Quenington church and there will be a special service of blessing for it this year on Sunday at the usual Family Service. Would parents encourage children to bring a toy or gift (not necessarily new) which can be offered at this service and later taken to bring pleasure to a Barnardo child at the Cheltenham home.

I wish you all spiritual joy this Christmas. G. S. Mowat

FAIRFORD

Lost: My precious 5 x 4 inch, leather covered, blue note book with streets and parishioners names written in sequence, which I have left somewhere over a month ago. I shall be very grateful if it can be found and sent home. E. Keble.

My Dear Friends

If I send any Christmas cards in Fairford this year it will be by hand for the sake of speed and cheapness.

In Fairford we have inherited our most beautiful church and as we all value it, and are proud of having it, so we ought all to do something as our share in maintaining its fair beauty. Some of its pinnacles are in immediate need of repair and towards this end the proceeds of the Christmas Fayre will go.

Mr Wally Fox was our Verger from 1949 until 1961. He devoted his time and gifts without stint to the service of our church. I have three outstanding visions of him in my mind. The first is Mr Fox some 75 feet above me in the church as he lay peering down from his horizontal position along side the rim of the opening in the top of the lantern tower through which a church bell may be lowered. He was fixing the Star of Bethlehem at Christmas time. Another time Mr Fox, small and rather frail of stature, came to unlock the iron gates of the church porch in the early morning. There he saw on the floor a heap of coats. Beneath them lay a man six feet in length. Before unlocking the South door, Wally sent him off good and sharp. On the third occasion he did complain gently. The water level in the boiler house below the church porch had risen more than usual after snow had melted. He asked if something could be done as now it was going over the top of his boots each time he went to stoke the boiler.

Edward Keble, Vicar

Edwardian Christmas card, very small in comparison with today's card. A scene of Highland cattle was a great favourite, together with embossed flowers – and not a sprig of holly!

Edwardian Christmas card; the recipient's initial on this one is embossed onto an attached, smaller card. Basic seasonal greetings are printed inside, but there is no pictorial reference to Christmas

Eastleach School Christmas play (date unknown)

MEYSEY HAMPTON AND MARSTON MEYSEY

In the October magazine I commented on the stability of the family life of the regular country dwellers because of their association with the world of nature around them, which season after season obeys the same laws, pursues the same objects and provides much the same results. It is quite interesting to look further into this and to relate it to Christmas. So if the world around you worships the family at Christmas time with all the usual excess and sentiment, which incidentally is but for the moment, let us Christians indeed acknowledge and return love with our own kith and kin but above all seek a birth of new insight into the mighty plan, purpose and love of God as related to the birth of the Baby at Bethlehem.

Meysey Hampton Septicentenary 1969. The plans have now taken shape and preparations are swinging into gear. Because of this there will be no New Year Social or Summer Fete.

Finally may I wish you all the very happiest Christmas and New Year.

Yours sincere friend Stephen Richardson

SOUTH CERNEY WITH CERNEY WICK

Organ Woodwork: We find that the woodwork of the organ frame at All Hallows has some woodworm. This could be very serious if it got further into the wooden pipes. Probably the only safe way to attend to this is to take the organ down, clean thoroughly and treat the woodwork. We have called for estimates for doing this work.

Your sincere friend and Vicar, P. Stacey Lewis

BIBURY WITH BARNSLEY AND WINSON

The light of the World: Soon the Christmas story in all its delicacy and wonder will again be unfolded. Its historicity may be denied by some, but few can deny the reality of its impact on the life of man.

Mr Edward Bennett gave a most illuminating description of the valuable Samuel Green organ in Barnsley Church. Active woodworm in part of this organ requires attention in the near future. Mr Bennett most kindly offered to initiate a fund for the restoration and resiting of this instrument, which would make it one of the finest Church organs in Gloucestershire.

My wife and family, and I, wish you all a very happy Christmas and every blessing and joy in the New Year.

D. Taffinder

THE EVE OF CHRISTMAS

By C. Henry Warren

Recording life and times in the Cotswolds, C. Henry Warren described it, as seen 'from one of its remotest corners', it is reasonable to assume that the year was that of 1935, as the book from which this extract is taken, A Cotswold Year, was first published in 1936 by Geoffrey Bles of Two Manchester Square, London. It has not been possible to trace either the original publisher or the copyright holder.

December 23

A 'bus ride in a remote country district is always an adventure, but never quite so much an adventure as just before Christmas. I was out in the heart of the Cotswolds and wanted to get to Cirencester, a journey impossible by train and only possible by 'bus if I could make two awkward connections fit in. All told it was under fifteen miles, but I shouldn't have bumped into such a variety of people in ten times that distance on a train. At all times rural 'buses are rare provokers of good fellowship: no matter how disgruntled the passengers may be when they get in, before they have got very far they have all been shaken up into such a mood of friendliness and good humour that they seem prepared to tell their neighbours almost anything about their private lives. But on a day like this, when Christmas is in the air, good fellowship is even more than usually rampant. The first 'bus I got into had been decorated behind the driver's seat with a couple of mistletoe sprays lavish with berries. I suspected the young conductor, for no doubt he was a wit. At one stopping-place in a village a young lady got in, smart in a townish sort of way that somehow didn't fit the scene. The buzz of conversation immediately stopped and everybody stared at her while she made her way to the only empty seat on the 'bus: it was just behind the driver and under the mistletoe. There was a suppressed giggle or two, and then the young conductor started whistling, '*If you were the only girl in the world,*' and winked knowingly at the rest of us. Everything was a joke to him. Even when one of the name-boards fell off the rack (where he had placed it none too securely) on to a passenger's head, he simply laughed and said, 'I'll let you off with a warning this time!'

The Adam and Eve in a snowy Paradise – the inn, at Paradise, near Painswick, is now closed

The second 'bus was no less festive, though I missed the mistletoe and the gay young conductor. Near me at one time sat a friendly old man who was very near the image of Mr Baldwin. A woman got in, whom he knew. She had on her head what appeared to be a clergyman's flat hat. My neighbour greeted her loudly and cheerily with: 'Good morning! How's the arm?' She paused on her way to her seat, clutched at the nearest support and glared at him. 'It was the foot!' she said indignantly. And when she was seated she launched on a tale of broken bones and accidents and funny feelings and sal volatile that lasted until she got to her destination. Two boys were having a fine time with a large electric bicycle lamp which they had just bought. It was so large and splendid that they simply couldn't resist flashing it on; so they shone it into one another's mouths to see how far down their throats they could see. Then there was the pale and serious clergyman who was being taken into the town by his wife to do some shopping. He was one of the shyest men I have ever seen and obviously embarrassed to find himself jostled about with such a loud lot of people; but his wife was quite oblivious to them. She was very concerned as to what money she ought to spend on almanacks and suchlike little gifts for the parishioners. Her husband tried to dismiss the matter as quite unimportant; he didn't like talking about such things in front of other people. I could see from his wife's insistent preoccupation, however, that a few pence more or less mattered a great deal. Theirs was the genteel poverty of those who have a reputation to keep up and nothing to keep it up on. 'You haven't thrown away the tickets have you?' she asked him presently, careful of everything by sheer force of habit. 'No, here they are, dear,' he answered meekly, pulling them out of the palm of his dingy suede gloves. And for the remainder of the journey they were silent, unable to bridge the barrier between themselves and their fellow-passengers, the only silent people in the 'bus.

December 24
When we got to Miserden, the village was shut in an intense darkness: no pointed junipers thrust their shadowy outlines against the sky and only an occasional lamp in somebody's cottage window declared that

not everybody was asleep. Most of the men folk of the village must have been in the Carpenters' Arms, so large an assembly filled the smoke-dense room when we opened the door. There must have been thirty men present, sitting and standing about, talking and laughing, while the landlord hurried in and out among them, throwing a joke over his shoulders as he attended to the orders fired at him from all quarters. A wood-fire filled the large open fire-place, over which there were arranged a row of bright brass candle-sticks and some shining steel spits. No game of darts monopolised the space and the conversation; no unsightly beer or tobacco advertisements spoiled the clean, washed walls; and instead of the usual smoky and inadequate oil-lamp a smart petrol-lamp threw abundance of light everywhere. I do not know a more attractive inn anywhere in the Cotswolds, and certainly I have never seen one so full of a jovial good-will as the Carpenters' Arms was this evening. Here were men who preferred sociable talk to silent drinks and games in a corner; even the inevitable 'oldest inhabitant', a man of eighty-six, mingled with the rest, his hand cupping his ear to catch the latest piece of local scandal and his eyes lighting up with pleasure as he bandied racy quips with his friends. Song after song filled the smoke-blue room, everybody joining in with gusto, and quite drowning the impromptu accompaniment of the fiddler, who wandered in and out among the singing crowd, shutting his eyes and sweeping his bow up to the ceiling. Now and then, one of the men would sing a solo, while the fiddler stood at his side and the rest of the company joined heartily in the chorus. One of the best songs tonight was a masterly performance of *The Barley Mow* and how good it was to hear this grand old folk-song removed from the artificial atmosphere of the drawing-room or festival and sung by men who have lived the sentiments they were singing! But perhaps my fancy was most seized by a ballad I had never heard before. It was sung by a middle-aged man whose absence of any tonal sense was more than compensated for by a rare vigour and naturalness. His ballad was all about a man who sailed abroad, taking with him a wonderful bird in a gilded cage. When he had settled down in his new country (obviously one of our colonies) the men used to gather about him to listen to the singing of that bird, their hearts almost ceasing to

A pipe meeting – possibly of the thirties – around the inglenook at the Mill Inn, Withington (original photo from The Mill Inn, photographer unknown)

beat at hearing again a thrush from their own far-away homeland … Too soon the landlord called 'Time, gentlemen!' For a while we stood outside the door, in the pitch-black night, tidying up the tag-ends of conversation, then made for home. 'Goodnight Bill! Goodnight Jack! And a happy Christmas!'

✦

Christmas

THE CHRISTMAS STORY COMES ALIVE

A Christmas Message from the Rt Revd Michael Perham,
Bishop of Gloucester

The Rt Revd Michael Perham tells the story of how the first crib was made by Francis of Assisi more than 750 years ago in Italy. The story that Bishop Michael tells is told more fully in Elizabeth Goudge's Francis of Assisi, *published by Hodder and Stoughton in 1961. Bishop Michael's story was published by* Cotswold Life *in the December 2005 issue, and is reproduced here by the kind permission of the bishop and by courtesy of* Cotswold Life.

St Francis had once been on pilgrimage to the Holy Land. All his life after he remembered – it was one of his most treasured memories – the night he had spent in the cave, for, in truth, it is more of a cave than a stable, in the little town of Bethlehem where Jesus was born. When he had knelt there in that cave, and imagined it filled with ox and ass, manger and straw, mother and child, he had felt so close to Jesus, that it really was as if he could see him and touch him, lying there as a baby. And now he wanted other people to have the same experience, not to think of the birth of Jesus as hundreds of years ago, but as something that actually happened in their own hearts at Christmas.

So Francis devised a plan. He was staying at a little hermitage where some of his brothers lived, near a little Italian village called Greccio. He had a rich and generous friend there and he went to him for help with his plan. His friend, Giovanni, built a stable in the woods outside the little town, next to the hermitage where Francis was staying with his

The Nativity as depicted in the medieval stained glass window in the north chapel of St Mary's church, Fairford (the world famous windows have now undergone major restoration and missing pieces – such as Joseph's head in this illustration – have been reinstated)

brothers, and he put a real manger in the stable and filled it with real straw, and next to it he built an altar for the Christmas Mass. He arranged that there should be a real ox and ass there on Christmas Eve. And he kept it all a great secret.

Meanwhile Francis sent invitations to all the local folk, the townsfolk of nearby Greccio and those living in the surrounding villages, inviting them all to come to the Christmas Mass at the hermitage. And an invitation from St Francis was not one to be refused!

They counted the days to the holy night and then they came. Down in the darkness of the valley, lights began to twinkle as men, women and children carrying lanterns and candles made their way towards the hermitage. And then you could hear them, for they sang as they came, singing a carol in honour of the Christ child soon to be born. It was a long climb and the singing had to stop during the steepest part, for they needed all their breath to climb. But, as they neared the hermitage, the singing grew stronger, until the first of them stopped in their tracks when they saw what awaited them, hidden in the woods close to the hermitage.

The crib – a tableau modelled in clay

The youngest got there first. The grown ups, a bit out of breath behind them, heard their high excited cries of wonder and joy, like the calling of birds, and a few came flying back saying, 'Father! Mother. There is a stable there. There is a manger for the baby, and an ox and an ass, a real ox and ass! And Father Francis is there. Hurry! Hurry!'

And so, when even the last had arrived, the Eucharist began, the Midnight Mass of Christmas. The wood became a church, and the stable the sanctuary. For, next to the manger, was the altar with the bread and wine and water. The lanterns were set on the ground or hung on the branches of the trees, and some of those who had brought candles still held them, and the flames lit up the faces of the worshippers, filled with the wonder and joy of it all.

Francis read the gospel to them. 'They came with haste, and found Mary and Joseph, and the baby lying in a manger.' And, as he read those words, they all turned to the real manger, in the real stable, and in their mind's eye, Jesus was there, Jesus was real, just like it had been for Francis when, those years before, he had knelt in the cave in Bethlehem and known that Jesus was there, Jesus was real.

The Nativity play – as enacted by schoolchildren throughout the kingdom

And then, a little later, when the priest at the altar held up the bread of the Eucharist and said the familiar words, 'This is my Body,' they felt that presence of the Lord all the more strongly. Yes, Jesus was real. Yes, Jesus was there. Yes, Jesus was born in their hearts all over again that Christmas. Francis was thrilled. His idea and Giovanni's hard work had paid off. The stable hadn't just been a bit of entertainment or just something pretty to look at. It had helped them to find Jesus, not so much in the stable as in their hearts.

That was the first crib, at least the first one we know about. The cribs you and I may see this Christmas probably won't be life-size. But they may serve to give us a sense of the mystery, the joy and the wonder of what happened in the stable and of the truth that God is with us, which is what 'Emmanuel' means. And Christian people who make their way to the churches at midnight or on Christmas morning and find themselves offered bread and wine may still sense that is a meeting place with the Jesus who is as real now as he was as he lay in the manger and as real as he was for Francis of Assisi when 1,200 years on, he knelt in the Bethlehem cave. I pray all that may be true for us.

THE CAMPDEN CAROL

A traditional carol arranged by Johnny Coppin

The following introduction by Johnny Coppin, Cotswold's own singer and songwriter whose many albums capture the essence of the region's rich heritage of folk song, poetry and culture, comes from his anthology, A Country Christmas, *published in 1996 by The Windrush Press. The Campden Carol features on his* West Country Christmas *album, produced by Red Sky Records, and is reproduced here by kind permission of Johnny Coppin.*

From Chipping Campden in Gloucestershire, this carol was handed down by word of mouth, probably from mediaeval times. I came across the words and a fragment of the tune in Gloucester Library, and together with Paul Burgess completed the melody. This carol is actually two in one: the first two verses were sung on Christmas Eve, and the last two for St Stephen late on Christmas Day in the evening. Both carols were sung to the same tune.

Rejoice, O man, for thy redemption signed.
The son of man, in pity to mankind,
Was of a virtuous Virgin born this day,
And the Blest Babe, within a manger lay.

'Twas strange that they, no room could find within
To entertain their Saviour and their King;
Who came from Heaven, for to redeem us all
From sin and death, entailed by Adam's fall.

Good St Stephen did a martyr die;
A crown of glory, he did gain thereby.
By suff'ring death, which proved to him, no loss,
Because he meekly bore his Master's cross.

And now in Heaven, in Heaven he doth remain
To wear a crown of glory, for his pain.
And every man shall have the same reward,
Who lays his life down, for his Lord.

Stanton in the
snow

CHRISTMASTIDE AT THE CHAPEL MINISTER'S HOUSE, DECEMBER 1860

By Sarah Thomas

Sarah Thomas was the daughter of the Baptist Minister of Fairford and Meysey Hampton chapels who, from her diary entries, was head of the household after her parents had died. Caring for her younger invalid sister, Kate, and half-brother, Charles, totally committed to the Baptist cause, overseeing the affairs of the two chapels, visiting the members and accommodating many visiting and travelling preachers, Sarah's diaries that have come to light cover the period 1860-65 – a crucial time in her life when, at the age of thirty-seven and still single, she is torn between which of two suitors she should accept. Her heart is clearly lost to John Davis, a Minister of the Baptist chapel at Arlington in Bibury parish, but despite his calling, Sarah has doubts about his total commitment to the church, finding his flirtatious ways with others difficult to accept.

Her other suitor, a widowed naval captain, was obviously away at sea during the Christmastide of 1860 as she does not mention him in these extracts from her diary over that period. Unlike most Victorian ladies' diaries and journals, Sarah's were not meant for anyone else's eyes. The entries are too frank and too revealing of her most inner thoughts that she could share with no other; they are, therefore, more a secret repository for her heartfelt feelings, but together with the struggle with her personal passions they give an intimate insight into the close-knit community of the chapel folk of the day. They also give a different aspect on the generally accepted picture of Victorian feasting and partying over the festive period. The extracts are taken from

The Secret Diary of Sarah Thomas (1860–1865), *edited by June Lewis and published in 1994 by The Windrush Press, with the kind agreement of the publishers.*

Friday 21 December, 1860
A busy day. Snow falling thickly. Randall called and he took me to Gower Street as he had business nearby, so I called on the Murphys. All pleased to see me. The horse omnibuses all full and the ground so slippery, Charles missed his footing on the step and mercifully escaped being run over by the wheels just in time. Kidd had called at Walducks while we were out so came again at nine. He was uncommonly free and said he would like to come for Christmas, but I didn't pursue it as I am hoping that John might come.

Saturday 22 December
After eventful journey with horses slipping with the omnibuses, we managed to catch the train on time and was so thankful to see Richard at Cirencester with the Coburg to meet us. Delighted to see my dear Kate again, and Emily says she will stay for Christmas.

Monday 24 December
While busy making mincepies, Mr Davis walked into the kitchen and was as usual. Kate in fun tried to make him think I hadn't come home and he looked dismal over it, but soon changed when he brought his wet boots into the kitchen and saw me there.

Christmas Day
It is very cold and frosty. The rime frost as thick as snow and presented a most exquisite appearance. Emily and I went into garden to see the trees. The elms in the orchard were lovely beyond description. The dark branches looked most rich with their foliage of snow-like feathers. Charles and dear John walked to Meysey Hampton in the afternoon and in the evening we had music and different games. It has been a merrier Christmas than we've had for years.

Hoar-frosted trees – part of winter wonderland

Norman arch of the ancient hospital gate of St Mary's Abbey, Cirencester, 1902

Wednesday 26 December
Mr Frise came over to wish Emily goodbye as she leaves tomorrow.
Mrs Frise came after and I was shocked to hear that she had heard at
Whelford that Milligan left his wife and children and went to Canada
and died. They lived a wretched life.

Friday 28 December:
The snow still beautiful, but sharp frosts make it very cold. The kitchen
all frozen up this morning. John again urged me to consent to his
proposal. He says he loves me more and more. He said he loves every
eighth of an inch of me three times over. We have had much fun with
him and Charles this week. Emily gave Charles a good tickling on the
floor twice, then John came into my bedroom before he left. I was so
vexed that Emily came and found him there. She said she wanted to say
goodbye and couldn't find us. She spoiled it completely for us as I felt
quite inclined to give way, but on reflection think it might have been
providential. Richard drove John as far as Coln and then he walked to
Arlington.

Sunday 30 December
Yesterday went to Cirencester and glad of warm wine at Keyworths.
Paid £250 into Charles's account, transferred from our own, then
withdrew £50 for our own expenses. After such sharp frosts the
weather has turned to torrential rain making travelling very dangerous.
The wet has come into our study like a flood and through the ceiling
into bedroom.

Tuesday 1 January, 1861
Last night Charles went to watch at eleven o'clock for the changing
year. I had called at Nanny's, then took flannel shirt to Francis's wife
and one to Paish's. Had but little sleep from ramping toothache and feel
middling today. Mr Cornwall made but a nominal visit. Poor old man,
he looked quite poorly.

Thursday 3 January
Had the Frises over for tea and had a romp with them in the hall.
Master Frank drank three glasses of homemade wine. (*Mr Frise was the
new Chapel Minister at Fairford after Sarah's father died.*)

Saturday 5 January
Charles, Kate and I tead at the Frises. They did all they could to make
us comfortable, but oh, the dirty little drabs of children. They were out
sliding until five and a half o'clock. Then, when they came in sat on
the hearth rug to have their tea, Jesse sopped his toast in his mug of
tea then put his dirty little paw, took it out and squeezed it dry, then
poked intinto his mouth. I could scarcely go on with my tea, it was so
disgusting to see the dirt running down between his fingers and into
his cup again. They are not managed at all and there was no peace until
they were all in bed. Mrs Frise made Kate a little cornflour pudding
and we supped round the fire. It was cold when we left and Mrs Frise
wrapped a big shawl over Kate's head and I carried her bonnet.

Monday 7 January
Yesterday was the first day set aside universally for special united prayer.
Went to prayer meeting tonight conducted by the Revd Mr Rice of
St Mary's in the Crofts Hall. The Methodists as usual made much noise.
Bought some warm petticoats for some old women at Meysey Hampton.

Wednesday 9 January
Bessie Booker called and so did Sarah Short, gave her warm wine and
bread and meat and a petticoat. Packed up mincepies and bacon for her
to take to her aunt.

Friday 11 January
Went to Cirencester as Mrs Tranter told me of a gardener, but I couldn't
stay to see him. We had a good warm at Richard's and a glass of grog.

Sunday 13 January
This has been a bad sad day for me. Everything has gone wrong.

Mr Davis does not come or write so I shall put him out of my mind as such worry hinders everything. There was extravagant talk at breakfast time which annoyed me, then I broke a bottle of rum and oil all over my dress and carpet. Elizabeth was very contrary and kept us waiting a long time for everything at dinner. I had to scold her thoroughly. I went to see poor Mrs Bedwell, she was very wandering and watched Martha so narrowly round the bed I fancied she wanted to speak to me alone. Gave warm petticoats to Hannah Vincent, though she be an old cat, Betty Miller and Marth Ecott. Snowed fast all evening.

Monday 14 January
It is the deepest snow we've had. Just as Kate and I had dined and removed the cloth a gentle tap at the parlour door made us jump. In

walked dear J, thoroughly tired and his feet wet. I felt reproached that he had walked from Arlington in the deep snow for my answer, for that is what he said he had come for. He said he was tired of suspense and if I didn't accept him he would go to Emily B. He said he wouldn't have much difficulty in obtaining her. He said she gave him quite a hint the other day. I was most vexed. I felt he looked dejected and didn't have the heart to say what I normally say to him that he must wait until I receive guidance.

Pickwickian style shops at old Cirencester

Wednesday 16 January
My romp with dear J appears to have cheered him up. I gave him some hot wine and then, in fun, I sketched him and Kate together with their arms round each other. He left at 4 and said he might come again in a month. I was sad when he left and had to resort to prayer as I'm so afraid of my own evil heart. Had to pull myself together as Mr Smith arrived and tead here, he came for his payment for preaching and I paid him £13 up to Christmas 1860. Then I felt annoyed with him as he is so determined to give children tea now, so Kate and I decided they shan't have books too. We wish they had books rather than tea, but he has already promised it to them. Kate cut open Spurgeon's almanack today.

Friday 18 January
Errands of mercy all day. Took a Dorcas shift to poor Jonathan Cowly's wife and found him alone, so took the opportunity of urging him to repent for his sins. Took worsted stockings to Thomas Simpson's, a child's shift to Mabbets and a pinafore for Shurmer's child. All were grateful.

CHRISTMAS IN A MONASTERY

By Father Charles Watson

Father Charles Watson spoke of how the monks at Prinknash Abbey prepared and celebrated Christmas in an interview for Cotswold Life *in 1996, when the monks were still in the ultra-modern (for the time) abbey which they have now left for a return to the original old manor to which he refers. Father Charles was talking to June Lewis and the feature is reproduced here by permission of the publishers.*

I have been at Prinknash Abbey since 1949. My first 23 years was in the marvellous old building which stands on the opposite hillside, such a beautiful old manor house in traditional Cotswold stone style. By comparison, this present Abbey is a ghastly looking building, but once inside the door we really appreciated having light and well-heated rooms, so irrespective of its appearance it is functional.

In its way, it also tells the story of the community here because the Brothers made so much of the furnishings, the stained glass, ironwork and choir stalls in the chapel, so it has a special feeling. We are a semi-closed Benedictine Order, but we do leave the Monastery on business from time to time and I go to see my sister, my only close relative, once a year and take the place of a parish priest in East Anglia when he takes his annual leave.

We are not entirely shut away from the outside world; we have one copy of *The Times* every day so keep abreast of the news. There is also a television set in the house and for special events we can record them. On some Sunday afternoons we may have a modern scientific film on, like the *Evolution of the World*. We do not, of course, have romantic films on!

It is strange how monks are imagined to be so serious all of the time. You wouldn't last long in a community so integrated as we are without a sense of humour. It belongs to our human side of nature, and if you can have a bit of fun and joy it helps, especially at such times as choir practice. It was wonderful to incorporate the audience in some plain chant when we gave the recital for the new organ and, of course, include *In a Monastery Garden*. I am an organ builder and musician by profession and studied at the Royal School of Church Music. When I first came to Prinknash, we had a French harmonium to accompany the Chant, and I said to the Abbot, who was then also the organist, that in a place like this we should have a proper pipe organ. He said we couldn't afford one, so I suggested we made one, and we did. It was quite small but it worked, with two keyboards – manual and pedals, and we were able to accompany the Gregorian Chant and play some Bach, it really was best for the music of the Baroque. If you have the desire to do something you are halfway there. I practise an hour a day on the organ, it is essential to keep it up.

Monks in Prinknash Abbey chapel

After I had built that first organ this building was not ready for its installation so during the year between, my organ went down to sing away at Gloucester Cathedral. It was used for many services and performed in *The Messiah* and broadcast several times. As a thank you, the Dean and Chapter presented us with a chalice and patten which we use every day at Mass so we have a wonderful connection, especially as Gloucester Cathedral was a Benedictine Abbey before the Dissolution. In the organ case are two carvings, done by a friend of mine, with the coat of arms of Prinknash and those of the last Benedictine Abbey of Gloucester.

Christmas will be quite hectic, there is always a lot going on. It starts with First Vespers at 4 pm on Christmas Eve, with a Service of Vigils about 11 pm, followed by Midnight Mass. That is always special and we have a fine Crib which we make ourselves. We decorate the house with holly and after Midnight Mass we meet in the Library for coffee and exchange Christmas greetings, so it is usually 2.30 am on Christmas Day before we get to bed, then we are back in chapel again for 7 am to sing the Service of Lauds, to be followed by Mass of the Day at 10.30 am.

We have a traditional Christmas dinner at mid-day, old-fashioned and made ourselves, everyone has already had a stir of the plum pudding on the first Sunday in Advent. This has become known as Stir Up Sunday from the Collect *Excita, Quaerimus Domine*, Stir Up we beseech Thee, O Lord. Latin is a beautiful language and that is probably why the church hangs on to it.

A Traditional Family Christmas

By Pam Ayres

In an interview for the My Cotswold Life *series in December 1995, Pam Ayres was talking to June Lewis. This extract is reproduced here by permission of Pam Ayres and the publisher of* Cotswold Life.

My Cotswold life at Christmas is totally involved in creating a traditional family Christmas. I never do pantomime or television or tours which will take me away from home over that period. Ever since I had my children I was determined that I should create the kind of Christmas they would remember and this is what we as a family enjoy.

Pam Ayres in her winter garden

Every year we bring down the shoe boxes overflowing with the years old baubles and bits. The boys always decorate the tree – the largest we can get into the house, and James adores tinsel so we have miles of glitter, then they seem to just stand back and throw it on to the tree. I just let them get on with it. It is for them, and childhood is so short that I can do all the designer stuff later on, with smart tartan bows and subtle lighting instead of flickering flashes which we have which drive you mad.

But then, we have all the lights in the room off – and the tree is transformed from an arboreal scrap heap to a thing of shining wonder, and viewed from outside this wondrous creation is quite magnificent framed by the window. William's birthday is a couple of weeks before Christmas, so we are careful about not letting preparations for Christmas advance into the aftermath of his special day.

I have such recollections of the arduous task of making the plum puddings which seemed to start about March and boil for ever in the old copper, that the pudding is about the only thing I don't cook now, but I make mountains of mince pies and lots of traditional dishes.

We have a big turkey and my dear old Mum joins us for Christmas.

Certain presents are early morning ones, the others are piled under the tree and we spend the afternoon opening them and the rest of the week trying to match them to the gift labels so that we know what to thank the givers for.

We go as a family to the carol concert at the boys' school and to one of the village churches, this sets the start proper to our Christmas, and adds to the warm anticipation and lovely atmosphere of the time. It is all this that the boys will remember. In my own career I don't spend time looking back.

CHRISTMAS AT HOME WITH MR AND MRS CHARLES DICKENS

By Stuart McHugh

Ivy Cecil Stuart McHugh, to give the great-granddaughter of Charles Dickens her full name, was the granddaughter of Charley, the eldest son of the great Victorian novelist. Charles Dickens's evocative pictures of Christmas past have endured the vagaries of literary fashion and remain the evergreen classic – as much a part of the Christmas of today as the holly and mistletoe with which we still deck our halls and more humble homesteads. In the following extracts from Stuart McHugh's writings of her illustrious ancestor she paints a more intimate picture of what life was like at Christmastide from family memories. As she wrote in the family notes prefacing the book, Mr and Mrs Charles Dickens Entertain at Home, *published by Pergamon General Books in 1970 – on which these extracts are based – Stuart McHugh's own Edwardian childhood was 'steeped in Dickensia and skilled reading aloud made the characters in his books utterly real, quotation* Household Words*'.*

Stuart McHugh, great-granddaughter of Charles Dickens; a portrait of her illustrious ancestor, as a young man, was a constant companion on her writing desk

Stuart McHugh lived in the heart of the Cotswolds and used many treasures of the Dickens family in her everyday life, and, as a special honour would allow close friends to sit on the great novelist's chaise lounge, or handle the precious scrapbook of sketches in which some of the characters were dressed in stuck on scraps of the material from the actual clothes they were wearing at the time.

These extracts based on Stuart McHugh's writings are reproduced here by the kind permission of her literary copyright heir, her grandson, Christopher McHugh — to whom I am extremely grateful. My thanks, also, for his permission to reproduce the delightful sketch made by his grandmother of Charles Dickens and John Leech dancing the polka with Mamie and Kate, Dickens's two small daughters. Stuart McHugh made the sketch from the cover of Mamie's book, My father as I recall him.

Charley, my maternal grandfather, wrote of his famous father, Charles Dickens: 'I am not at all sure that the first recollection of my father was not more derived from tradition than actual memory. Indeed, as I had at the time (relating to the Christmas of 1838) attained the ripe age of two or thereabouts, I suppose it must have been so. But I do remember very well one Christmas Day dinner at Doughty Street when, owing to the non-appearance of one of the guests the party consisted of thirteen and I was brought down from the nursery to fill the gap and afterwards set on a footstool on the table close to my father at dessert time. It was one of his few superstitions, by the by, this thirteen at the table.'

Christmas was a very important family occasion to Charles and Kate Dickens. Kate always had the table looking bright and pretty and the food presented in the best Christmas tradition. The pudding was set on its own special dish of coloured *repousse* china, ornamented with holly and it came in with the brandy alight and flaming.

A CHRISTMAS CAROL

By Charles Dickens

Mrs Cratchett left the room alone, too nervous to bear witness to take the pudding up and bring it in. Halo! A great deal of steam! The pudding was out of the copper. A smell like washing day! That was the cloth. A smell like an eating house and a pastrycooks next door to each other with a laundress next door to that; That was the pudding. In half a minute Mrs Cratchett entered, flushed but smiling proudly with the pudding like a speckled cannon ball, so hard and firm blazing in half of half a quarten of ignited brandy and bedight with Christmas holly stuck on top. Everybody had something to say about it, but nobody said it was at all a small pudding for a large family. Any Cratchett would have blushed to do such a thing. Bob served out the hot stuff in the jug and proposed a toast. 'A Merry Christmas to us all my dears. God bless us', which all the family echoed.

'God bless us every one,' said Tiny Tim, the last of all.

Mamie, sister of Charley Dickens, wrote of her father:
My father was the fun and life of Christmas gatherings for he loved to emphasise Christmas in every way and considered that the great festival should be fragrant with the love we should bear one another. Long walks with him were daily treats to be remembered. Games passed our evenings merrily, 'Dumb Grambo' was a favourite and one in which my father's great imitative ability showed finely. I remember one evening his dumb showing of the word 'frog' was so extremely laughable that even the memory of it convulsed Marcus Stone, the clever artist, when he tried to imitate it.

Charades and country dances of home made invention were strenuously performed. The finale was usually the Sir Roger de Coverley, danced very much in the same manner as old Fezziwig's Ball in the *Carol*.

Charles Dickens wrote that his son Charley's twelfth birghday party was, 'very merry'. Stuart McHugh recorded the fact that as well as conjuring for the party, dressed in a Chinese costume and wearing a very large mask, the great Dickens demonstrated the then new dance, the polka.

Charles Dickens, on the right, dancing the polka with his little daughter, Mamie (sketch by Stuart McHugh, and reproduced here by courtesy of Christopher McHugh)

Charles Dickens and John Leech, some 6ft tall, danced with Mamie, who was not yet ten years old and Kate, some eighteen months her junior, as their partners. Mamie recalled in later years how her father was so determined to perfect the steps of the new dance that he had forsaken his warm bed in the middle of the night just before the party and practised the steps in bitterly cold by rushlight! Learning to dance was one of the lessons that Dickens insisted on for the children at an early age and showed great interest in their prowess.

CHARLES DICKENS'S PUNCH
(MAKES ABOUT 3 PINTS)

Charles Dickens's Punch Party included Christmas cake, mince pies, assorted sandwiches, Victorian Shrub (a rum punch) and his own specially devised punch bowl.

Peel into a very strong common basin (which may be broken, in case of accident, without damage to the owner's peace or pocket) the rinds of 3 lemons, cut very thin, and with as little as possible of the white coating between the peel and the fruit, attached. Add a double handful of lump sugar (good measure), a pint of good old rum and a large wine glass full of brandy – if it be not a large claret glass, say two. Set this on fire, by filling a warm silver spoon with the spirit, lighting the contents at a wax taper and pouring them gently in. Let it burn 3 or 4 minutes at least, stirring it from time to time. Then extinguish it by covering the basin with a tray, which will immediately put out the flame. Then squeeze in the juice of the 3 lemons, and add a quart of *boiling* water. Stir the whole well, cover it up for 5 minutes, and stir again.

At this crisis (having skimmed off the lemon pips with a spoon), you may taste. If not sweet enough, add sugar to your liking, but observe that it will be a little sweeter presently. Pour the whole into a jug, tie a leather or coarse cloth over the top, so as to exclude the air completely, and stand it in a hot oven for 10 minutes, or on a hot stove one-quarter of an hour. Keep it until it comes to table in a warm place near the fire, but not too hot. If it be intended to stand 3 or 4 hours, take half the lemon peel out or it will acquire a bitter taste.

The same punch allowed to grow cool by degrees, and then iced, is delicious. It requires less sugar when made for this purpose. If you wish to produce it bright, strain it into bottles through silk.

The Dickens's Yuletide festivities culminated with entertaining at New Year, and a move of house in 1851 brought a note from the prolific author that he could not work on his new book as everything was 'topsy-turvy'. A month later he wrote, 'I am beginning to find my papers and to know where the pen and ink are'.

Charley wrote of his father always writing, 'with a quill pen and blue ink; never with a lead pencil. His manuscripts were written upon white 'slips', though sometimes on blue paper. On the shelf of his writing table were many dainty and useful ornaments – gifts from his friends or members of the family, and always a vase of bright fresh flowers'. (*Stuart McHugh always kept his favourite vase on her writing desk, too.*)

The size of the order that the butcher was asked to deliver was such on one occasion that he thought he should mention it to Kate Dickens in case there was some mistake, but as Charley wrote in explaining the need for so much food that they entertained so many guests at their homely 'theatricals', playing 'to an audience of ninety for three nights at home. At the first supper for the performers and guests, Lord Campbell declared that he would rather have written *Pickwick* than be Lord Chief Justice of England'. Lord Campbell was, in fact, the Lord Chief Justice of England – famed as a law reformer and an author of important works on matters of law.

A Kate Dickens Menu for a party of 18-20 people

Pea Soup
Broiled Salmon. Turbot
Lobster Sauce
Cucumbers

Mushroom Patties
Lamb's Fry
Lobster Curry
Rissoles
Roast Saddle of Mutton
Mayonnaise of Chicken
Broccoli. New Potatoes. Peas
Roast Duck

Pudding. Clear Jelly. Italian Cream

Macaroni Cheese
Brunswick Sausage

Kate Dickens's book, *What Shall We Have for Dinner*, from which this menu was taken, was published in 1852. It was no doubt a reference to her husband that she wrote of 'Sir Jonas' as not a gourmand but a man of discernment and very knowledgeable about culinary matters; he certainly conjured up all manner of food in his novels, from workhouse gruel to the most lavish feasts. It comes as something of a surprise, therefore, to find Charley writing of his father's eating habits, 'I wonder for how many years his breakfast consisted of a rasher of broiled ham; how many dinners were begun with a glass of Chichester milk punch; how many were finished with a dish of toasted cheese; for he was conservative in his personal arrangements.'

A DICKENS OF A COTSWOLD CONNECTION

Although there is no evidence of Charles Dickens having set any one of his numerous works in the area, there are a couple of stories where, reputedly, a character or a circumstance was based on historical fact in the Cotswolds, although the delightful picture drawn up by the great novelist's pen of Pickwick and friends singing duets in the dickey, after they had wined and dined at the Hop Pole in Tewkesbury, is specific and memorable.

Scrooge, the infamous character in the perennial classic, *A Christmas Carol*, is generally thought to have been based on Jemmy Wood, acknowledged as the world's greatest miser. Wood ran Gloucester's Old Bank on Westgate Street and tales of his miserly habits are legion and legendary, including his beggarly routine of picking up stray knobs of coal from Gloucester Docks for his own fire. When he died in 1836 he was officially declared a millionaire – an incredible status to have achieved in those days. Dickens's *A Christmas Carol* was published a few days before Christmas 1843 and has been enshrined in the moral and nostalgic spirit of Christmas ever since.

Bibury Court, a gracious and gabled Tudor mansion house, is a Cotswold idyll. Set in spacious grounds through which the clear waters of the Coln run along the valley, it presents a picture of rural peace and tranquillity, which J. Arthur Gibbs, who lived just a short walk away, described in his *A Cotswold Village* a century ago, 'a view we would gladly have walked 20 miles to see'. Built in 1633 by Sir Thomas Sackville, an illegitimate son of the 1st Earl of Dorset, was a Knight in waiting in the court of James I, and Bibury Court remained in the family for several generations. Through the female line it passed to the Cresswells which eventually resulted in a tangle of intrigue over a disputed will and years of litigation. Charles Dickens is said to have had this protracted court case in mind as the plot for his *Bleak House*, in which there has been such renewed interest.

There is certainly nothing bleak about this beautiful house that was sold as a result of the Cresswell court case. Since 1968 it has been a highly acclaimed country house hotel: Kate Dickens would have approved of its most recent Christmas Day menu – her own extensive collection, published under the nom de plume, Lady Maria Clutterbuck, wife of Sir Jonas Clutterbuck, was a gastronomic revelation of the Dickens family dinner table.

Bibury Court, viewed through winter-bare branches

CHRISTMAS DAY DINNER, 2005

At Bibury Court Hotel

———————

A Selection of Canapes

Amuse Bouche

Ballottine of Foie Gras, Moscato Jelly, Toasted Brioche OR
Diver Caught Scallops, Jerusalem Artichoke Puree and Madeira

Truffle Risotto, Cerney Crayfish Brochette, Perigeaux Black Truffle

Church Hill Farm Roast Goose, Pot Roasted Vegetables, Cranberry
and Orange Jus OR
Crisp Roast Seabass, Lobster Beignet, Basil Crushed Potatoes, Shellfish
Bisque

Homemade Brandy and Vanilla Yoghurt, Christmas Crumble

Assiette of Chocolate OR
Blueberry and Lemon, Caramelised Wafers OR
A Selection of British Cheeses, Celery and Chutney

Mince Pies

CHARITABLE FOOD

By Charles Dickens

It was the goose (and the plum pudding, of course) that was the focal point of the dinner in A Christmas Carol, *but Charles Dickens features turkey and beef in this extract from the story he set in a charitable shelter for six homeless souls; each of whom paid fourpence for a night's poor lodging. As the seventh traveller, he provided a Christmas Eve dinner, after which each person told a tale of his own choosing.*

I went back to my Inn from Watt's Charity to give directions for the Turkey and Beef, and could settle to nothing for thinking of the poor travellers advancing on their resting place along various cold roads. Upon the stroke of nine I set out for the Charity, carrying my pitcher of Wassail in my arms. Following me in procession came:

Ben with the Beer
Inattentive Boy with hot plates

Second inattentive Boy with hot plates
The Turkey
Female carrying sauces to be heated on the spot
The Beef
Man with tray on his head, containing Vegetables
and sundries
Volunteer Hostler from the Hotel, grinning and
rendering no assistance

We passed along the High Street comet-like, and left a trail of fragrance behind us, which caused the public to stop, sniffing in wonder. So soon as the wall-eyed young man we had left in the yard should hear the railway whistle, always carried by Ben, he was to dash into the Inn kitchen seize the hot plum-pudding and mince pies, and speed with them to Watts Charity, where they would be received by the sauce female, who would be provided with brandy in a blue state of combustion.

All these arrangements were executed in the most exact and punctual manner. I never saw a finer turkey, finer beef, or greater prodigality of sauce and gravy; and my Travellers did wonderful justice to everything set before them. It made my heart rejoice to observe how their wind and frost hardened faces softened in the clatter of plates and knives and forks, and mellowed in the fire and supper heat. While their hats and capes and wrappers, hanging up, a few small bundles on the ground in a corner, and in another corner three or four old walking sticks, worn down at the end to a mere fringe, linked this snug interior with the bleak outside in a golden chain.

CHRISTMAS DAY IN THE WORKHOUSE

Written by George R. Sims, 1879

It is Christmas Day in the Workhouse
And the cold bare walls are bright
With garlands of green and holly
And the place is a pleasant sight
For with clean washed hands and faces
In a long and hungry line
The paupers sit at the tables
For this is the hour they dine

And the guardians and their ladies
Although the wind is east
Have come in their furs and wrappers
To watch their charges feast
To smile and be condescending
Put pudding on paupers' plates
To be hosts at the Workhouse banquet
They've paid for – with the rates

These are just two of the eight-line verses which George R. Sims wrote to bring what he considered pious hypocrisy of feasting and making merry at Christmas in the workhouse to public attention. There are a further twenty verses in which Sims, a journalist who was a vigorous campaigner against poverty, railed against the guardians appointed under the Poor Law who regarded themselves more as guardians of the rates, instead of adequate provision for the poor. A typical Victorian euphemism was to call the workhouse a House of Industry, as at Fairford, but by any other name, conditions were harsh and the express intention of the 1834 Act was to ensure that life in an institution would be considerably worse than that endured by the poorest labourer – including the segregation of family units, loss of personal freedom, a strict regime of manual and menial work, uniformly dressed in drab clothes and existing on a meagre and monotonous diet. No wonder that reports on the festive fare punctuated the pages of the Union log books and local newspapers in such glowing terms to allay the conscience of any rate payer who might have given a thought to the less fortunate who found themselves in that desperate situation.

The last of the old Knights of the Road – the tricycling tramp pauses in Macaroni Woods in the early seventies

The House of Industry – Fairford Workhouse, around 1815 from a sketch by Miss A. Keble

A random glance at some of the Cotswold workhouses at Christmas reveal much about the same pattern. In 1849, the guardians of Winchcombe Workhouse stipulated that no more than a sovereign should be spent on providing the inmates with a Christmas dinner 'and extras'. At Dursley, the workhouse master was allowed £4 5s for providing, 'a better diet than usual on Christmas Day and a goose for the officers' in the 1870s. Cheltenham board of guardians stipulated that the inmates at Christmas 1904 should have half a pint of beer with Christmas Dinner, and the same at 10 am on Boxing Day!

By 1892 tobacco and snuff were allowed to elderly men and there was extra tea allowance for elderly women. Local benefactors were encouraged to make charitable gifts to the inmates, and there appears to be some gentile competition at Winchcombe in 1895 when Mrs Adlard of Postlip Hall donated tea, tobacco and cakes to the festive table; Mrs Emma Dent of Sudeley Castle not only matched Mrs Adlard's bountiful fare but added sugar, sweets, oranges and nuts to her Christmas hamper. Stow-on-the-Wold workhouse fared rather better in 1900 when Mr Ormerod of Oddington added a number of dolls and toys for the children to the general presents of oranges, sweets and tobacco distributed, and the band of the Company of Volunteers visited, 'the house and played a selection of music to the great delight of the inmates'. The Poor Law of 1929 saw the last of the workhouse system after more than ninety Christmases had been spent in the sixteen institutions in the old county of Gloucestershire.

THE JUBILEE BOY'S CHRISTMAS

By Richard Martin and Judith Fay

Capturing conversation in print while compiling a biography that is more than a story of one man, but embraces that of a village and that of a time, is an achievement that Richard Martin and Judith Fay realised in their fascinating book based on notes made and long chats to George Swinford of Filkins. In fact, George could have been easily dubbed as Mr Filkins – so much a part of its life and fabric was he for over a century, starting from the year of Queen Victoria's Golden Jubilee, hence the title.

These extracts from The Jubilee Boy, *by Judith Fay and Richard Martin, are but small slices from the whole cake of social history from which the reader is drawn to 'cut-and-come-again' as George Swinford himself might have said. They are reproduced here by kind permission of Richard Martin and the publisher, the Filkins Press.*

Every Christmas Squire Fox's mother at the big house at Bradwell Grove gave all the women a Christmas box. There is an entry in the School Log Book, dated 11 December 1896, 'A great many children away this afternoon chiefly because their mothers are gone to Bradwell Grove for gifts.' You could choose if you would have sheets or blankets or a dress length. Mother always chose material. The one thing she wanted was a sewing machine, that was what she had *got* to have, and she was going to get it even though it cost five pounds. Of course Father had not got five pounds, so she worked for a farmer, haymaking and harvesting, and she saved that five pounds and got her sewing machine. A Singer treadle, it was. She was sewing every night after dark, and my sisters had to do a bit too. We only had candles for a long time. It was wonderful when we got our first paraffin lamp.

The Rummage Sales were exciting places those days. The women used to fight each other over the dresses. Mother was always collecting pieces for her rag rugs, and one day Squire Fox's hunting coat was in the sale. There was a good scramble, but Mother got it, and after that there was always a piece of red in the middle of each rug, and sometimes in the corners too. We also had the gold buttons – WHK they had on them, for William Henry Fox. Lovely buttons they were.

Squire Fox's father Samuel Fox invented Paragon umbrellas. They were the first ones with steel frames, the ones before having cane or whalebone frames. His factory was in Sheffield. He must have made a mint of money out of those umbrellas. It was said that he left three hundred and three thousand pounds in his Will. Squire Fox's mother was very good. She would invite the women of Filkins, Shilton and Bradwell Grove to go to tea with all the young children. We had a lovely tea party, bread and butter, cake and lettuce (lettuce was very special). Then at six o'clock the butler would bring in the beer in copper jugs. After that they would start walking home, chattering and singing, with the babies in the prams and the older children walking beside. We used to wonder why some of the women fell down on the way back.

Another big day of course was Christmas – and how different it was when I was a small boy. How we looked forward to hanging up our stockings, and how excited we were with the contents, which were an orange, a sugar mouse, a sugar pig and a penny tin whistle or trumpet. For breakfast we had bacon fried with half an egg and mashed potatoes, for dinner ham and vegetables and plum pudding; for tea we had salt buttered toast and cake, and for supper ham again. All this food was very special, and different from usual. We had one book in our house, *The Family Herald* I think it was called, and on Christmas Day we were allowed to see the pictures in it, we thought this a great honour. In the evening we sat round a nice fire and roasted crab apples on the hot bars of the grate and ate them with nuts. I would mention that in the autumn we used to go and get crabs, take them home and fill a box, put them under the bed and keep them until Christmas. We also gathered hazelnuts and beechnuts, which had to be kept in tins so the mice could not get at them.

On Christmas Day we always had to go to Sunday School, and marched in line to church. When we came out the teachers marched us to the vicarage, in single file. At the door stood the Vicar and his wife, and as we passed by each one had a penny and an orange. As I got older I used to go round singing carols, and collected a few coppers. If the weather had not been too bad and Father had not been out of work, or if the fat pig they had just sold had done well, we could buy some extras, but it was not very often we got away from bacon.

George Swinford at cottage door in Filkins

Mostly we ate home cured lard instead of butter as long as it lasted, but we could buy salt butter for one shilling per pound at the farm. You could see the salt in it when you cut it, and it was very good for toast, and that is what we enjoyed for Christmas tea. Later years we used to have a football match on Christmas Day, which was very much appreciated after the Christmas dinner. Now there is nothing doing except a walk.

We had Sunday School at school, not in the church. The teacher came back on Sunday and you had to go, even if you were Chapel people. The schoolmaster was the church organist. It was all church in those days. The name of the school is Filkins-cum-Broughton. The parson came down nearly every day to give us our scripture lesson. We had to learn the Collect and a verse of a hymn. We got three marks on the register – one for attendance, one for the Collect and one for the verse. These were counted up at the end of the year, and perhaps you got a prize. When we were old enough we had to go into the choir, which meant we had two services on Sunday and practice on Friday night. When we attended, it was marked on the register and we received a halfpenny, which was paid out at Christmas. If you misbehaved at any of the services, the parson would say 'Swinford, you will be docked.' This meant you lost your halfpenny, and if it occurred very often he would go and see our mother and tell her to give us a thrashing, which she obeyed.

We had a good choir then, all the choir stalls filled with men and boys, and seats in front for the girls. Certain people had their own seats, and no one else was supposed to use them without permission. The sexton was very strict, and not particular about giving you a clout on the ear if you were talking or laughing. We always kept our eye on him.

The Christmas of my Childhood

By John Moore

This extract from Country Column 1959 is reproduced by kind permission of the copyright holder, The John Moore Society.

Our Christmas was on a large scale, not because we were particularly well off or had inherited obligations, but because my father was, most of the time, Mayor of Tewkesbury, and was also head of a firm of auctioneers, and we lived in a big house in the middle of the town, and my parents were known for kindliness and generosity.

So our Christmases were a bit Dickensian. Stupendous quantities of food were prepared against the needs of all sorts and conditions of people. Hundreds of mince pies. For some reason which I have never understood, all the wives of the railwaymen (they were no special responsibility of ours) were taken mince pies in the week before Christmas and I used to trot round beside my mother when she performed this little charity.

Then there were all the drovers, porters and hangers-on who worked for my father's firm; and the clerks in the office; and the town's functionaries who served my father when he was Mayor, and the poor, who in those days if you lived in the middle of a country town, were close and real and pitiful and menacing. My father always gave them money at Christmas, only little sums, sixpences and shillings, which they spent on booze. My mother (as any woman would) thought they should have food instead, lest they spent the money on drink. But my father held Dr Johnson's view – why not?

Old-time cooking demonstrated at
Cogges Edwardian farmhouse

'It is surely very savage to refuse them every possible avenue to pleasure, reckoned too coarse for our own acceptance. Life is a pill which none of us can swallow without gilding; yet for the poor we delight in stripping it still barer.'

This civilised attitude explains why Old Cookie was never sacked, though every year on D-Day minus 40, she got drunk, blind drunk, utterly sozzled, on the Christmas pudding rum. And, of course, as Christmas came nearer, she would have more and more of these little lapses. And on certain days there'd be no cooked lunch, or an improvised dinner, and the whisper would go round the household: 'Old Cookie is on the rum again.' But next day she would seek forgiveness, perhaps with a Christmas cake – three feet in diameter, orange flavoured sponge with layers of thick cream, and a top icing as thick as snow on the eaves in an old-fashioned Christmas card, white frosty icing with 'Master John and Miss Daphne' inscribed in orange with a still shaky hand, candied orange slices all the way round the edge of it.

Then 1914 came, and I was seven, and the Uhlans were riding through Belgium, and there were no more orange Christmas cakes, mince pies by the hundred, free ale for the drovers, whole legs of beef, saddles of lamb, 15 pound turkeys, geese for those of the office staff with more than five years service, bottles of port for the Town Crier, glasses of brandy in the kitchen for Old Cookie. The curtain fell upon all those things. But before it fell I'd had my brief glimpse of an old-fashioned Christmas which seems to us now almost unbelievably Dickensian.

A VICTORIAN RECTOR AND NINE OLD MAIDS

By Michael Boyes

The Revd Robert Le Marchant was rector of Little Rissington for over fifty-two years. The fact that of his fifteen children, his nine daughters remained spinsters all their life seems to have been accepted by him, and them, with equanimity although of concern to their mother, brothers and better-off relatives, whose generosity was often tapped to keep up the necessary appearances of the rectorial family. Michael Boyes skilfully weaves together excerpts from letters and diaries, journals, photographs and living memories of villagers to form a rich tapestry of this extraordinary family within the broader context of social and economic fabric of the time in which they lived. His book, A Victorian Rector and Nine Old Maids: 100 Years of Cotswold Village Life *– from which these extracts are taken – give a glimpse of some of the ways in which the daughters enjoyed the isolation and rigours of winter, and how they carried on with their father's parochial duties well into their own old age at Christmas.*

Little Rissington village under snow (Photo: courtesy Michael Boyes)

Eight of the nine Le Marchant spinster sisters (Photo: courtesy Michael Boyes)

Reproduced from A Victorian Rector and Nine Old Maids: 100 Years of Cotswold Village Life *(2005) by Michael Boyes, by kind permission of the author, and the publishers, Phillimore & Co Ltd, Shopwyke Manor Barn, Chichester, West Sussex PO20 2BG.*

During the long periods spent at home in Little Rissington, the sisters occupied themselves in a variety of ways. The last quarter of the nineteenth century witnessed a tremendous growth in team games for women and the Le Marchant sisters were amongst the first in the north Cotswolds to take advantage of this new trend. Their knowledge of sport was extensive, and they could impress guests by telling them when the Derby was won in a snowstorm. In winter when the weather was cold enough the sisters loved to skate and they often walked to Gawcombe pond where, in January 1894, the ice was nine inches thick. Sometimes they walked several miles to Upper Slaughter where the Revd Francis Witts had built a shallow skating lake. They regarded themselves as adept skaters 'five members of the family were cutting all kinds of figures on New Bridge pond', wrote one of them in December 1886.

At Christmas the Le Marchant family presented villagers and their children with a variety of gifts and toys. The children assembled on Christmas Eve in the schoolroom, where they were given a festive tea. Afterwards they gathered around a Christmas tree to receive their gifts, each one carefully chosen. In 1911 Mrs Streatfeild Moore, the new lady of the manor, considered the presents to be 'magnificent'. After the rector died his daughters continued to give Christmas presents to all the villagers until the Second World War. 'They ran their own social service for the village,' commented Eddie Butler. 'They each took responsibility for a number of families, visiting them if they fell sick and bringing them food if necessary. They must have had a pretty good bush telegraph to tell them when families were ill.' And when Jaffa oranges were in season they would deliver one to every household in the parish.

Sometime before Christmas each of the daughters would call on their adopted families to ask the children what they would like. Then

Little Rissington church, seen from the Rectory window (Photo: courtesy Michael Boyes)

they would hire a taxi from Jack Minchin to take them to Cheltenham and return with the car full of presents. If necessary, they would make several journeys. 'I always asked for a book and used to get an annual or a compendium of stories,' said Eddie. 'They delivered their presents to each house just before Christmas, with a roll of cloth for the women and socks or gloves for the men,' said Stan Collett, 'and my present was usually a fretwork set or a Meccano set.' Every year Bill Oakey received a Chatterbox Annual and a football from Miss Flo, whilst Miss Nellie gave David Lane something useful such as a vest or socks. 'The Le Marchants were a brilliant family,' said Donald.

Unto Us a Child is Born

By Diane Harris and Tracy Spiers

The following memories are taken from the book Stroud's Birthplace *by Diane Harris and Tracy Spiers, in which mothers (a more appropriate term than patients) recall Christmastime in Stroud Maternity Hospital. They are reproduced here by kind permission of the registered copyright holders Diane Harris and Tracy Spiers (2003). The book was compiled to mark the half century of service to the area and to raise funds towards the hospital's bid to gain the UNICEF and World Health Organisation's Baby Friendly Hospital Initiative, a global campaign to establish best practice in breastfeeding.*

Stroud Maternity Hospital Staff have always made Christmas special. In the early 1950s, Christmas Day babies used to be put in a decorated crib and on every cot there was a stocking with presents for mother and child – usually made by the staff. It was the matron's job to decorate the tree and her enthusiasm to create a festive atmosphere was infectious.

Margaret Hamilton recalled: 'I spent Christmas in the hospital because you stayed in for ten days then. I've still got the little card they put on the end of the cot. I was in the hospital at the same time as another mother whose surname was Christmas.

I had never been in a hospital before and husbands were not allowed in so he didn't see Ian until the day after his birth. He wanted to call him Oscar and he did for quite a while, but I thought it was a dreadful name!'

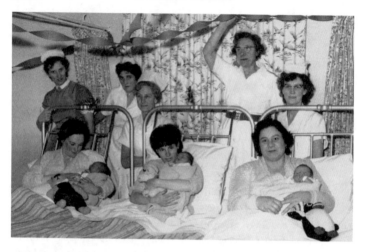

Mums in Christmas ward at Stroud Maternity Hospital (This and the
following two photographs courtesy of Diane Harris and Tracy Spiers from
Stroud's Birthplace)

Carol-singing choristers in corridor

Nursery Nurse June Strange recollected that Christmas was a big, big thing. 'My children would come in, be shown round and be allowed to peep at the babies, and matron would always have a present for them on the tree. Those of us on nights on Christmas Eve would put little stockings on every cot and a present for the mother on the bed.

When I started at Stroud there was a sister who wanted us to sing carols on Christmas morning, so the four of us would dress up in capes and wake the mums up by singing carols. One year, this sister decided that instead of singing she would bring in a wind-up gramophone which we put on a trolley. It was my job to switch the record on. I remember pushing this thing through the double doors and switching it on, but what I didn't realise was that it was on double or treble speed. I'll never forget *Christians Awake, Salute the Happy Morn* sounding like Pinky and Perky and seeing all the mums shoot out of bed with their curlers in. The sister looked at me. She wasn't amused, but then the mums all started to laugh and we doubled up. I was teased about that for a long time.'

Nursery Nurse Ann Durn remembered: 'On Christmas Eve we had turned our capes inside out and walked down the long corridor to the main ward holding a candle. One time I remember one of the nurses crying as we did so. She was a Roman Catholic and wanted to marry someone who wasn't and her parents wouldn't let them. She was very upset. I guess the singing made her quite emotional. I felt so sorry for her.'

Sister Mavis Cossham recalled: 'We used to have a crib which was all trimmed up with lace at Christmas, with its own hood. The League of Friends gave a silver spoon to any baby born on Christmas Day and we made the babies a garment or toy to put in their Christmas stockings. This was usually done during our coffee breaks. Dr Crouch used to carve the turkey and gave the mums a drink. The choir from Trinity church came round and had mince pies afterwards. The Christmas lunch was made by Mrs Adams, who was a brilliant cook. It was real home cooking. Marvellous.'

Joy Thacker's first baby, Katrina, arrived on December 17, which meant Christmas in hospital in 1969 which she described as 'a memorable, magical experience. Looking back, I realise much of this was due to the atmosphere within the hospital. On the days approaching Christmas

Day I watched as the matron, Miss Light, balanced on a stepladder and dusted beams before draping the decorations over them.

There were carol singers on Christmas Eve and Christmas Day, and staff sang us awake in the darkness of Christmas morning with candles and presents, many of which they had made themselves. Those of us who were allowed up ate Christmas lunch at long trestle-tables, and the meal was presided over by doctors in fancy hats, one of whom carved the turkey. There was even a glass of wine. In the afternoon, a special Christmas tea was served to mums and visitors alike. The mum in the bed next to me had no visitors, so staff shared this time with her to make sure she was not left out.

Boxing Day morning brought its own excitement because I was going home. Before I departed, the League of Friends arrived with presents for the babies and mums. Katrina received a miniature blue Wedgwood cup and saucer and I got some toiletries.'

Laurie Lee, playing his guitar to wife Kathy and baby Jessy

Another vivid memory was the babies mewing like kittens as they were wheeled into the ward, in their blue and white shawls, on long trolleys.

Laurie Lee's daughter, Jessy, was also born at Stroud Maternity Hospital. Kathy Lee contributed her feelings for the special place. 'The matron of the hospital at the time, Marion Light, was Laurie's cousin so it was all in the family. She was wonderful. You couldn't have a better midwife. She was very efficient. I was 32 and considered old in those days to have a first baby. I think I stayed in Stroud almost a fortnight. Jessy weighed 7 lb 2 oz; just a nice weight, not too big. Laurie wasn't at the birth.

I have always loved the hospital. It is beautifully run and everyone I know has been happy there. I have been inside the hospital since and it is still lovely. To even think of closing it would be madness.'

Memories of the incomparable Marion Light, who was matron from 1961 until her retirement in 1983, centre round her love of Christmas.

Frances Light, Marion's sister, said: 'She was responsible for all aspects of the administration of the hospital, including seeing the cook each morning to plan the menu. There was a large kitchen garden with two gardeners who would bring in fresh vegetables daily. Marion was very dedicated and well thought of, judging by the number of cards and good wishes she received on her retirement. She officially retired on December 21, 1983, her 60th birthday, but was able to stay until December 25 because she loved Christmas Day and all the preparations. She had previously worked at Gloucester City Maternity Hospital where a great deal was made of Christmas and decorations. She followed in that tradition.'

Among the many tributes paid to Matron Light by doctors and nursing colleagues, Sister Freda Bishop recalled: 'In the bad winters, Miss Light would walk from Sheepscombe and still be at work for 7.30am. She was a bundle of energy and always running about. Laurie Lee was her cousin and he went to the hospital at Christmas with his guitar and entertained everyone.'

Nursing Auxiliary Teresa Lautieri had vivid memories of her. 'Miss Light was not as regimental as Miss Haskins, but she was a very hard working woman. For the hospital's 25th anniversary she made a stork out of papier mache and we all had to help break up the bits of paper.

At Christmas she made choirboys out of empty egg shells, bottles and crepe paper and lined them up on one side of the short corridor joining the two longer ones. They all had little faces, frills and books. Decorating the Christmas tree was her job. One year she did let someone else do it, but then she re-did it afterwards! We were allowed to decorate the Christmas cot and the nursery, but she didn't trust us to decorate the corridors and the wards.

We always went to a pantomime for Christmas and once we went by coach to Cardiff. We were supposed to take a large mince pie with us but had left it in the kitchen. We were sitting in the theatre when in came Miss Light, wearing her red and blue cape and clutching this mince pie. She had followed the coach all the way to Cardiff in her car. We couldn't stop laughing. She was an eccentric who had to look after everybody.'

CHRISTMAS

A Poem by W. H. Davies

Acclaimed as one of Britain's greatest Nature poets, W. H. Davies lived the last years of his life at Nailsworth, delighting in the simple joys of Cotswold country life, many of which he captured in the lines of his poetry. 'What is this life if, full of care, we have no time to stand and stare' has become one of the most quoted philosophical maxims, perhaps even more pertinent in today's mad rush-around world than when he penned the lines in 1911. In this poem, 'Christmas',

the theme of making time for reflection on its true meaning, and enriching life by
celebrating the festive season among 'all kinds of men', follows along similar lines
to his famous 'Leisure'. It is reproduced here by kind permission of the copyright
holders of Mrs H.M. Davies Will Trust.

Christmas has come, let's eat and drink –
This is no time to sit and think;
Farewell to study, books and pen,
And welcome to all kinds of men.

Let all men now get rid of care,
And what one has let others share;
Then 'tis the same, no matter which
Of us is poor, or which is rich.

Let each man have enough this day,
Since those that can are glad to pay;
There's nothing now too rich or good
For poor men, not the King's own food.

Now like a singing bird my feet
Touch earth, and I must drink and eat.
Welcome to all men; I'll not care
What any of my fellows wear;

We'll not let cloth divide our souls,
They'll swim stark naked in the bowls.
Welcome, poor beggar: I'll not see
That hand of yours dislodge a flea, –

While you sit by my side and beg,
Or right foot scratching your left leg.
Farewell restraint: we will not now
Measure the ale our brains allow,

But drink as much as we can hold.
We'll count no change when we spend gold;
This is no time to save, but spend,
To give for nothing, not to lend.

Let foes make friends: let them forget
The mischief-making dead that fret.

The living with complaint like this –
'He wronged us once, hate him and his.'
Christmas has come; let every man
Eat, drink, be merry all he can.
Ale's my best mark, but if port wine
Or whisky's yours – let it be mine;
No matter what lies in the bowls,
We'll make it rich with our own souls.
Farewell to study, books and pen,
And welcome to all kinds of men.

Christmas tea party at Fairford Pop-In Club, date unknown – possibly late seventies (Photo: Wiltshire Newspapers)

CHRISTMAS FARE

By June Lewis-Jones

Now thrice welcome, Christmas,
Which brings us good cheer,
Minc'd pies and plum porridge,
Good ale and strong beer;
With pig, goose and capon,
The best that can be,
So well doth the weather
And our stomachs agree.

The unknown author – probably the most prolific of all poets, Anon – who penned this little rhyme lists the traditional festive fare that spells Christmas in all home-lovers' hearts. For some families, Christmas fare meant little change from what they survived on throughout the year – again, it was often the family pig that was the salvation. Christmas tradition demanded that there should be something a little different, however, and sucking pig became that something special. Keeping a full litter stretched the meagre budget, so it was deemed more economical to kill a piglet of about six weeks old for the festive feast. The meat is very rich but delicate and it was elevated from a poor peasant's make-do meal to become the centrepiece of a celebratory feast. Roast pork, roast beef, goose, cockerel and turkey have changed with the swings of fashion in food over the years as the main dish of the Christmas dinner, but mince pies and plum pudding remain customary; even so, these old favourites have undergone some subtle changes.

Mincemeat did, until Edwardian times, actually contain minced meat; since then, only the inclusion of beef suet is an echo of earlier mince pies; now, the vegetarian and healthier version of mincemeat is made with vegetable suet. Mrs Beeton's recipe for mincemeat in her *All About Cookery*, published in 1901, includes both lean beef and beef suet along with the usual dried and citrus fruits and, of course, the copious quantities of brandy.

CHRISTMAS PUDDING: FROM PLUM PORRIDGE TO COTSWOLD FEGGY DUMP

Plum porridge predates mince pies and has its origins in Tudor kitchens. A concoction of beef and veal, boiled in spiced wine, usually hock or 'old sack', to which citrus fruits, fried, dried plums and dried grapes, sweetened with honey, were added before thickening with crumbled coarse bread to a porridge consistency, was served in bowls to be eaten in a semi-liquid state. The rich pottage later became a filling in pastry cases as oven cooking became more accessible, and so was born the mince pie.

Plum pudding, which we now know as Christmas pudding, derived from the plum porridge – and takes its name from the time when all dried fruits were collectively called 'plums'. In Cotswold dialect, dried fruits were known as 'feggy', often thought to mean figs, but as figs did not often feature in the plum pudding, it is more likely that they referred to dried prunes (also called plums, just for confusion).

Stirring the traditional wish into the Christmas pudding at Farmor's School in the seventies

By the mid-eighteenth century meat was omitted from the plum porridge; just the suet fat was used and the mixture was thickened with a higher proportion of breadcrumbs and solidified with a little flour. The whole was then rolled into a large ball and boiled in a cloth – easier to do if the mixture is heaped onto the cloth, then, using the cloth, shaped into a ball and tied tightly. It was the latter-day Victorians who put the pudding tidily into a basin and covered the top with a cloth, tying opposite corners across in a knot to make an easier to manage handle.

Keeping faith with its origins, a Cotswold Feggy Dump (Christmas pudding) still has twice the weight of breadcrumbs to flour, to keep the pudding light in texture, though heavy with fruit. The addition of a grated carrot makes it more crumbly and using brown sugar and black treacle darkens the pudding, but the deep colour comes really from the long, long boiling time.

A glance through some old recipe books shows how little the basic Christmas pudding has changed over the last hundred years, and such was the confidence in the stability of prices with which Mrs Isabella Beeton wrote her *All About Cookery* in 1901 that the book includes the cost of each recipe.

Mrs Beeton's Menu for a Christmas Dinner for Ten Persons, 1901

Gravy Soup was made from 6lb shin beef, a 5lb knuckle of veal, two slices of nicely flavoured ham and a mixture of vegetables: it took seven hours to make.

Russian Salad was a mixture of cold, cooked vegetables, anchovies, any cold, cooked fish, olives, mayonnaise sauce and aspic jelly.

Mrs Beeton's Very Good Plum Pudding, 'seasonable on the 25th December and on various festive occasions till March', comprise the basic ingredients of dried fruit, breadcrumbs, etc and a wineglassful of brandy, was costed at 4s; her Unrivalled Plum Pudding with more fruit, pounded bitter almonds, sixteen eggs and half a pint of brandy was priced at 7s 6d, and a Plum Pudding for Children, minus the tipple, could be made for 2s.

A handwritten recipe in an old exercise book, belonging to Fanny Morse, dated 1927 and headed *Royal Christmas Pudding,* specified Australian currants and sultanas, South African raisins, Canadian apples, Old English beer and a gill of rum.

A local 'catering establishment' notebook dated 1942 gives an interesting insight into the costs and strict economy imposed by war-time restrictions.

Christmas fare in the inglenook

CHRISTMAS DINNER, 1942
FOR 400 PERSONS

Roast Pork with Sage and Onion Stuffing and Apple Sauce
Roast Potatoes and Greens
Christmas Pudding and Custard

Pork 85 lb @ 1/6d		£6 7s 6d
Gravy 60 pints @ 1d		5 0
Apple Sauce 50 lb @ 7d		1 9 2
Stuffing:	30 lb bread @ 2d	5 0
	30 lb onions @ 5d	12 6
	Sage, salt and pepper	3 2
Greens 100 lb @ 3d		1 5 0
Potatoes 2 cwts @ 9s		18 0
Christmas Pudding 30		3 15 0
Custard 52 pints milk and water		9 4
3 lb 4 ozs Custard Powder		3 3
3 lb 4 ozs Sugar		1 1
Vanilla essence		3

Total, including 66 and 2/3rds per cent, came to £26 14s 8d
Notes: Cost per head 1s 3d and a halfpenny
Tickets cost 1s 4d and included tea or coffee. All tickets sold on the five preceding days. All pork was not available and some top side of beef was served.

450 meals were served altogether – a great success.

CHRISTMAS PUDDING, TO SERVE 100 PEOPLE (1942)

4 lb each of flour, bread, grated raw carrot, grated raw potato, and suet

2 lb each of sugar, raisins or dates, currants or prunes, sultanas, figs, marmalade and black treacle

1 tablespoonful each of ground mixed spice, ginger and nutmeg

8 dried eggs

4 pints milk and water

1 pint beer

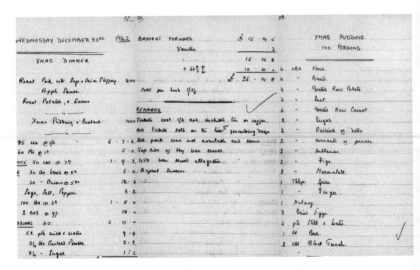

Three pages from war-time catering notebook

FARMOR'S SCHOOL COTSWOLD CHRISTMAS PUDDING, TO SERVE 460 CHILDREN (1977)

Making the traditional Christmas pudding in the kitchen of Farmor's School was a mammoth task, and teachers and a number of sixth formers would be invited to have a stir and the customary wish.

1 stone each of breadcrumbs, flour, suet and margarine mixed and dark brown sugar
23 lb dried fruit (a mix of raisins, currants, sultanas and dates)
9 lb apples, peeled, cored and grated; 4 lb lemons (use grated rind and strained juice)
14 large carrots, grated; 38 eggs; 5 lb marmalade; 4 ozs pudding spice; 2 lb treacle
4 teaspoonsful each of bicarbonate of soda, baking powder and almond essence
4 level dessertspoonsful salt
Milk and water, sufficient to mix to a soft dropping consistency.

Keeping the Christmas Dinner tradition alive!

By Ralph Jones

My family severed their long-established London roots, after living through the long blitz years of the Second World War, to settle in a farm cottage at Field Barn, near Tetbury. It was rural bliss, full of the adventures a schoolboy enjoys with fields to ramble and the ever-changing seasonal work going on at Farmer Foxwell's farm. Quite isolated from the nearest village or market town, my parents, surprisingly for city folk, took to the more primitive conditions with the spirit of young pioneers. Dad cultivated the large cottage garden and mum, my sister Heather, and I foraged the hedgerows for crab apples and blackberries that mum turned into really tasty puddings and jam cooked on an old, black kitchen range. There was no electricity to the cottage and water came from an erratic system from the farm; winter evenings were particularly cosy, reading or playing board games on the kitchen table in the pool of light from the Aladdin lamp.

The garden seemed to have a never ending crop of vegetables, but when it came closer to Christmas the brussel sprouts were watched over carefully and all kinds of things dangled and swung around on strings of baling twine in an attempt to keep the pigeons away from them so that we had the traditional sprouts on the great day. We still had ration books which were in use for the first year we were at Field Barn, and like most people in the early fifties, we relied heavily on our home grown food; and, being in the countryside, rabbit stew and rabbit pie were regular features.

Ralph and Heather Jones enjoying the snowfields at Field Barn in the early fifties (Photo: courtesy Lilian Jones)

Lilian and Hector Jones with their daughter, Heather, cutting the ice (Photo: courtesy Lilian Jones)

Christmas was special and that meant a cockerel for dinner. Dad's pride and joy was his fifty or so chicken that supplied us with lovely brown eggs, and the occasional casseroled hen that 'had gone off laying', but the cockerels meant Christmas dinner. The Indian Game cockerel was magnificent with its almost exotic plumage and Dad kept threatening it with sage and onion stuffing – as it had the nasty habit of flying at his ankle and giving it a sharp dig with its ferocious beak. But it was the Rhode Island Red that he favoured with extra food with an eye on it for the Christmas table. Then, one day, a couple of weeks before Christmas it keeled over in the run, its eyes hooded and its beak opening and shutting in a pathetic manner. Dad, who was in the ambulance service in the immediate post-war period of blitz-torn London, was well used to acting calmly and quickly. He carried the unconscious cockerel into the house and laid it on the kitchen table; making a deft incision in the poor bird's wrinkled neck he then slit open the bulging crop, swiftly emptied it of the mass of corn with which it had gorged itself into a stupor then called on my mum to thread a needle with strong cotton – and calmly stitched it up. After a couple of days of careful nursing back to health, the cockerel was returned to the run and seemed to take on a new lease of life. It was a life short-lived, however, as, come Christmas it ended up on the dinner table: my Dad had upheld the tradition of the countryman's policy of not letting a bird or animal die before it was killed; and we had our traditional Christmas dinner.

A CHRISTMAS AT THE ROUND HOUSE

By Elizabeth Speller

More like an island or a boat, the Round House sat on the confluence of three waterways: the Thames, the Coln and the derelict Thames-Severn canal. Arriving for Christmas was both exhilarating and challenging. The river seeped into the very stones of the building and winds lifting off the water howled round the tower like something from a Gothic novel. The only concessions to modernity were the eventual replacement of hazy gas mantles with an unreliable electricity supply; as a result, the cottage was frequently, and dangerously, lit only by candles. While we waited for the cottage to warm up, bed with several hot water bottles and dogs became irresistible. You could tell if the rudimentary boiler had gone out in the night by the icy tip of your nose on Christmas morning and the fern-like frost patterns on the inside window panes. Even excited children were inhibited from coming down to check whether Father Christmas had come, presumably by boat, until an adult had lit the fire.

We were always, and excitedly at the mercy of the elements. One Christmas floods spread as far as Lechlade church spire – more Noah's Ark than nativity scene – and we rowed over the fields to fetch our huge turkey from the Lechlade butchers. On another, a heavy frost turned the water meadows into a Christmas afternoon skating rink with the skaters sustained with hot punch.

Each winter we would cut one of our own Christmas trees and stand it in the window. Sometimes, returning home on foot along the

The Round House, Inglesham (Photo: Elizabeth Speller)

towpath with the house invisible in the dark, there were the lights of the tree, seemingly suspended over the river, a new constellation in the night.

The Round House was a world in itself: a white, icy world, tucked away beside the murmurings of the infant Thames, and the best of all places for a magical Christmas.

My Best Ever Christmas Present

By Ellie Jarvis, aged fourteen

When I was five, my Mum used to tell me about her beautiful doll that she had when she was my age, a lovely talking doll called Rosebud. I used to sit down with Mum and we'd play with my dolls. When I was bored of this, I used to ask Mummy about her dolls with such an air of fascination, like I couldn't believe that it was real – Mummy was never ever little like me … she must be making it up! But Mummy would tell me about Rosebud and all the things she used to say, such as: 'I love you, Mummy!' and 'Please may I have a biscuit?'

None of my dolls talked, and none of them walked, like a doll I had read about in a favourite Enid Blyton. I decided that I wanted a doll just like this, and I asked my Mummy if she still had Rosebud. To my disappointment, the answer was 'No'.

But Christmas was not far off, and when it rolled round, I opened all my presents with the glee that a little child always has at Christmas, comparing mine with Ed's presents, and smiling and praising his toys, but always thinking: 'A *gun*! Why would he want one of those? Mine are so much better!' Or, if he had something that I liked, sitting quite still, just watching it, coveting it … or sneakily picking it up when he wasn't looking. But the last present I opened was big, and rectangular – a big box. Eagerly, pulling off the wrapping, I found a box containing a beautiful doll, lips slightly apart with big brown eyes and glossy brown hair. I was in raptures – it was the most beautiful doll I ever had! Mum told me to press her gently – I did, and though I couldn't be happier, I

Katie Jarvis watches Ellie, Miles and Edward opening their Christmas presents
(Photo: Katie Jarvis)

was, as to my delight, she remarked: 'My name is Rosebud. May I have
a biscuit?' I hugged her so hard, and I still have her to this day, sitting
ever so politely with her big brown eyes, dutifully repeating everything
I tell her to say.

LETTER TO SANTA

From Miles Jarvis, aged ten

Dear Santa

I think you are really great and kind as you deliver presents to children all over the world. While we're on the subject of presents, this Christmas coming I really want a Nintendo DS and also Thanks for the presents last year (special the robo-raptor).

I've had an exspeariance of you before. It was last Christmas 25/12/05, I was wide awake because I could not get to sleep by now it was about 1.30 am. So I went down stairs to the kitchen where my Mum was finishing off work, so I told her that I couldn't get to sleep and Santa wouldn't come. Then Mum told me, 'Why don't you do what Edward once did. Get your pillow case and put on the landing, after that, shut the door.' So that is what I did, then about 2.00 am I heard footsteps, then my pillow case and presents rusling is what I heard next. One part of me made want to open the door and look at you in the landing lit by a light in the corner, but the stronger part said, stay, wait, don't move just lisen.

Not just me many people have exspearinces of you like my brother (Edward) one Christmas he heard banging on the roof then look down at a present full pillow case, also my best friend Imogen once repeated taps on the roof then she looked out of the window and there was nothing there?!

From

Miles

Dear Santa,

I think you are really great and kind as you deliver presents to children all over the world. While we're on the subject of presents this christmas coming I really want a nintendo DS and also Thanks for the presents last year (special the robo-raptor). I've had an experiance of you before. It was last christmas 25/12/05, I was wide awake because I could not get to sleep by now it was about 1:30 am. So I went down stairs to the kitchen where my mum was finishing off work, So I told that I couldn't get to sleep and santa wouldn't come. Then mum told me, "Why don't you do what Edward once did. Get your pillow case and put on the landing, after that, shut the door."

So that is what I did, then about 2:00 am I heard foot steps, then my pillow case a presents rusting is what I heard next. One part of me made want to open the door and look at you in the landing lit by a light in the coner, but the stronger part said stay, wait, don't move just lisen.

Not just me many people have experiences of you like my brother (Edward) on christmas he heard banging on the roof then look down at a present full pillow case, also my best friend Imogen once repeated taps on the roof then she looked out of the window and there was nothing there?!

From
Miles

Letter to Santa (Miles Jarvis)

Katie Jarvis with Miles, Ellie and Edward on the Gloucestershire/
Warwickshire Santa Special Express (Photo: Katie Jarvis)

CHRISTMAS BY NO OTHER NAME

The Place-Names of Gloucestershire, edited by A.H. Smith, published for the English Place Name Society by the Cambridge University Press 1963-4 lists only one entry for Christmas as a place name, and that is in Bristol – at the time when that city was included in Gloucestershire county. A summary of the entry is as follows.

Christmas Street dates back to 1484 when it was spelt as *Cristemastrete*; and as *Crystesmastrete* in 1512, derived from Middle English *crist(es)masse* 'Christmas', but the circumstance of its use here is unknown; it was possibly a street associated with the custom of the festival; but Christmas was a well-evidenced Middle English byname and this is undoubtedly the likelier usage here.

Christmas Court is an ancient courtyard containing specialist shops in the High Street at Burford in the Cotswolds.

A Cotswold Father Christmas and Family

Anthony Christmas who was born and brought up in Stroud, and his wife, Jean, became a real Father and Mother Christmas when their daughter, Jacqueline, was born – on Christmas Day! 'Jacqueline was the Christmas baby born in 1953 – in the first year that Stroud Maternity Hospital opened,' recalls Jean. 'With a surname like ours, we resisted giving our little girl a Christmas-related name, like Holly or Mary'.

Santa Claus figure as
developed from the
American Coca-Cola
advertisement

'I used to get teased about being called Christmas when I was a boy,'
Anthony said, 'but there are a few of us Christmases in the Stroud area
– all related, but I don't think there are many others in the Cotswolds.
It isn't such an unusual surname, though. I remember that *The Sun*
newspaper, in what I am sure was the first year that they started,
invited everyone with the surname of Christmas to a party they put on
specially for us. Over a hundred Christmases turned up, but mostly they
came from the London and South-East region. They put on a proper
Christmas type party, with a decorated tree and mincepies and the like
– even though it was held in the mid-summer!'

A Child called Christmas

The following extract from Genealogical Miscellany *in the May 2006 issue of* Family Tree Magazine *is reproduced here by kind permission of the Editor.*

Reference some months ago to certain popular (and unpopular) days upon which people married – or had their children baptised – has rung a few bells. Alison Pascoe, emailing from Cheltenham, has a six-times great-grandfather, John Hallier and his wife Martha (nee Cooper) who had 18 children from 1723 to 1741 at Wickwar in Gloucestershire. There seems no pattern to the days upon which the first seven were baptised, but the next five were all baptised on a Christmas Day, including a child called Christmas (in 1733).

Christmas for all Seasons at The Christmas Shop

Wrapped in winter woollies, or sun-hatted and sun-tanned, people come throughout all seasons to gaze at the wonderland of winter's special festival forum at The Christmas Shop at Lechlade. The first Christmas shop to open in the Cotswolds, this magical mecca is celebrating its twenty-first anniversary this year, and Judy Hurt, who now owns the shop, says that she has sold something every day she has been open; to a collector, a Father Christmas figure is not just an annual symbol of custom, but an all-year-round character and different styles are eagerly sought after. Baubles, boxes and bows hang from Christmas trees dripping with delightful decorations, mostly hand made in Europe and as far away as Kashmir. Crafting Christmas decorations has never been a particularly English art, although we now start promoting Christmas much earlier than our European cousins, but it was the way that Germany, in particular, celebrated the festival in such a traditional manner that impressed Alison and Colin Dawes, that prompted them to found the business over two decades ago. Their love of Christmas is shared and perpetuated by Judy, who says that everyone that goes into the shop is happy; no matter what age they are, they absorb a little of the magic and many overseas visitors make it an essential return visit.

A Christmas toy shop of the thirties, from the author's scrapbook

Everything has its own little story of origin from often quite remote corners of the globe, but when it comes to seeking out a traditional English Santa, it comes as a surprise to learn that he was originally a green figure of ancient woodland folk until the beginning of the twentieth century when he appeared in the now familiar scarlet short jacket suit and boots with snowy white beard, following an American Coca-Cola advertisement to jolly up the festive trade; the traditional English style is still a long cloak or coat. Today's children also identify more with engines than reindeer drawn sleighs, and it is Santa in a train with three carriages that attracts their attention in this virtual Aladdin's cave where the magic of Christmas is captured all year round.

Dr Henry Stephens wears the traditional English Santa's long red coat for his duties as Father Christmas at Fairford Cottage Hospital

The Christmas Shop, open all year round at Lechlade

Storytelling: Ghosts and Legends

THE STORYTELLER'S TALE

Told by Chloe from the Midnight Storytellers

Christmas is the traditional time for telling tales, and the art of the storyteller is the stuff of legend itself. From the Greek muses through civilisations and cultures to the romantic Elizabethan minstrels and on to the more earthy and regional re-telling of half-forgotten truths in half-remembered folk songs, tales have been told of lives and loves, passion and power, and any goings-on that went on of note, in an unbroken line of oral history. Despite the impact of on-screen entertainment in the twenty-first century, the storyteller still holds centre stage in our desire to be transported into the 'once upon a time'. We are fortunate in the Cotswolds to have the Midnight Storytellers upholding that tradition, weaving their own magic into our cultural heritage. Chloe gives us an insight into just what being one of the Midnight Storytellers means to her at Christmastide.

Every Christmas I sense relief rising off my audiences like steam from a plum pudding. While you listen to a story, whining children and demanding mothers and the whole miserable debt-inducing race to shop, cook and shop again for the Big Day do not exist.

In the world of story, Christmas snow lies deep and crisp and even. Wolves howl in the approved manner, forests are satisfyingly mysterious. Ugly women become beautiful by the power of love and kindness (a magic that works in any world). A beggar discovers the meaning of generosity. And it doesn't matter how fake my Baboushka accent is, people laugh when she scolds the Magi and hearts melt when she offers the newborn Prince of Peace all the trinkets she'd gathered for the children she never had.

Traditional stories carry the identity of nations, the memories of communities, myths, legends, folk tales. This worldwide heritage contains powerful and moving reminders about what it means to be fully human. Morals and messages underlie every tale. Thoughtless choices have results you can't imagine, or control. Beware what you wish for – you might get it! At the same time, every listener interprets the tale in their own way.

Storytelling is a spontaneous art form. No scripts, no reading out of a book. The storyteller is like a jazz musician – following a theme; drawing on artistry, tradition and adrenalin to make magic.

Christmas audiences can be merry, sour or stodged to the ears with festive fare. I have to assess quickly if the telling needs to be crisp and light, rich and romantic, or just over and done with as fast as possible!

Chloe, a Midnight Storyteller

There's a fashion among modern storytellers for self effacement. Modest voices, plain attire, 'ego' and theatrics disdained. I believe this is an insult to audiences. If people have paid to be entertained, it's my job to deliver the goods for their eyes as well as their ears.

All year round I go for glamour. At Christmas the serious glitter comes out. Little black dresses, wild child evening wear (pink or peacock!) with swirling duster coats, red and green and mega-sparkly earrings and bracelets. Glitter eye shadow, bright lipstick. And, of course, the leopard-spotted or scarlet high heel boots. It's the middle of winter; it's England; people are in desperate need of cheering up!

In the Cotswolds, one audience can contain a mind-bogglingly mixed bunch: from fusty professors to shiny IT experts to tweedy young WI ladies. Invariably there are weary, wind-blasted farmers. Two golden rules apply: Do Not Get Between An Audience And Their Food; and, Don't Start Later Than Nine Thirty. Cotswold people work hard and drive long distances; come evening, they don't appreciate being kept waiting for supper. By 9.30 p.m. they're sleepy, energy for listening dwindles, and I've learned to wrap up by 10.30 p.m. at the latest.

I lost my heart to the Cotswolds when I was eight years old. It's a privilege to live here, and to work at what I love. Doesn't matter if it's a cosy country inn or a cruise liner-sized hotel all chintz and no taste. Doesn't matter if it's a glittering dinner party or a rickety village hall in some hamlet that's not even on the map. Faces light up with joy and wonder, the atmosphere swirls with dreaming and laughter. Those winter tales and festive fables hold a power which calls to the true spirit of Christmas in everyone.

So, next November and December, I'll be finding my way in the pitch dark, nursing my poor old car down ancient lanes, in gusts of rain, bouncing through puddles with potholes as deep as Australia. There's be skies quivering with stars, the smell of frost, bare branches against the moon. Several nights a week I'll be coming home to hot chocolate, happy cats and (the secret of comfortable country life) my electric blanket!

It is very special to be a storyteller in the Cotswolds at Christmas.

CHRISTMAS AND COCKCROW

Y.J.B. Partridge, published in Gloucestershire Countryside,
Christmas Number, 1939

*As the magazine no longer exists, it has been impossible to trace the author of
this article.*

Because the Christmas story begins in a stable, the favourite live creatures
of farm and cottage have been drawn into a charmed circle of popular
imagination. In the spirit of Italian Primitives, the ox and the ass were
drawn upon our church walls; oxen knelt in the English barton; bees sang
in their hives. One of the most interesting traditions belongs to cockcrow.
The Spectator of Steele and Addison, issued on Christmas Eve, 1709,
begins thus:

> 'The time of year puts me in mind of those lines of Shakespeare,
> wherein, according to his agreeable wildness of imagination,
> he has wrought a country tradition into a beautiful piece of
> poetry. In the tragedy of Hamlet, where the ghost vanishes
> upon the cock's crowing, he take occasion to mention its
> crowing all hours of the night about Christmas time, and to
> insinuate a kind of religious veneration for that reason.

> > Some say, that ever 'gainst that season comes
> > Wherein our Saviour's birth is celebrated.
> > The bird of dawning singeth all night long;

And then, they say, no spirit can walk abroad;
The nights are wholesome; then no planets strike,
No fairy takes, nor witch hath power to charm;
So hallow'd and so gracious is the time …

Of all the birds and beasts, the cock was nearest to the spirit-world. Before Christianity was, and after, he had power over witches, ghosts and all evil things that walk by night. He was more than that: next to the sun, moon and stars, he must have been the oldest time-keeper in the world. His hours were not the hours as we know them, at intervals of sixty minutes; he knew only the pre-Conquest 'tides' with three-hour intervals, such as King Alfred marked on his candles and the Catholic Church still observes in the Canonical Hours – 3,6,9,12, by night and day. The cock was expected to do, for the night and early morning, what the scratch dial on the church wall did for the hours of sunshine. Neither dial nor cock ever marked a 'tide' at 9 p.m. when every respectable man should be in bed and asleep.

A winter's tale told by the old kitchen range in a Daglingworth cottage

Midnight was the 'First Cock'. The foul fiend Flibbertigibbit 'begins at curfew, and walks to the first cock', which scared him back to the lower world. Three o'clock in the morning was the 'Second Cock'. The servants in Macbeth's castle were 'carousing till the second cock', when Macduff's summons came knock-knock at the gate. Mr Keith Henderson (who was one of our Cotswold artists before he moved to the Highlands) told me that, before the days of watches, when herring boats went out from Barra, in the Outer Hebrides, they used to take on board with them a cock, because it would be sure to tell them when it was three o'clock in the morning and time to turn homewards. The 'Third Cock' was just before daybreak – too well-known to dwell upon further.

In his time-keeping, the cock was held to be as true as the Abbey clock. Before Christmas, however, there came a change; the cock ceased for a while to tell the hours; his work became wholly spiritual, keeping at bay the powers of darkness. Therefore he sang all night long, according to the 'country tradition' which Shakespeare has preserved for us, though, strange to say, no one has yet found out Shakespeare's authority

What real foundation (if any) is there for all these notions based on the cock's mysterious sense of time? So far as observations can prove, these birds (like geese, game birds, and moorhens) may call occasionally at any hour of the night, more frequently after midnight than before, and chiefly, of course, to herald the dawn. It is mere wildness of imagination to tie them down to the 'Tides' or hours. But for a few weeks before Christmas, roughly corresponding with Advent, cockcrow in the dark hours comes much more often and is much greater in volume. Our forefathers may well have thought that the bird of dawning, always endowed with uncanny knowledge, bore witness to a 'hallow'd, gracious' time. For when Christmas (or the Christmas market) is over, many of those voices have been silenced, and cockcrow comes with such long pauses that spirits once more dare walk abroad through the winter night.

THE LADY MAUD

By Adin Williams

Kempsford is a strong contender for the most haunted village in the Cotswolds with Lady Maud being the most famous of all its ghosts; the story dates back to the days of the Plantagenets when the barons were in opposition to Edward II. The tragic tale is almost Shakespearian in its dramatic intensity and has long been locked into the folklore of the area, kept alive by generations of local people who have, or known someone who has, sighted the ghost of Lady Maud as she makes her wraithlike way through the centuries still haunting the river bank where she met her violent end at the hands of her jealous and misinformed husband. The high banked path alongside the Thames in the grounds of the Old Vicarage is still known as Lady Maud's Walk, and the small stone building at the end of it, where she hid her husband's brother – a fugitive from the civil battles – still stands in melancholic isolation, a romantic ruin shrouded in its own mystery and history. During the last war, the local Home Guard ensured they patrolled Lady Maud's Walk in pairs – the prospect of encountering the Lady of the Mist, as she is known locally, was obviously more scary than that of finding any enemy infiltrator canoeing his silent way along the dark Thames waters.

Adin Williams was master of the village school at Kempsford so the story was very local to him and he retold it in an incredibly long poem in his book, Lays and Legends of Gloucestershire, *printed by Savory's Steam Press of Cirencester. And, contrary to what Shakespeare indicated about ghosts not walking abroad at the hallowed time of Christmas, Lady Maud is legendary in keeping 'a nightly tryst', so while the good folk of Kempsford tell her tale in the comfort of their smoke-shadowed inglenooks, the lady herself still walks and*

Lady Maud's Walk at Kempsford, showing the ruins of the river room alongside the bank (from an engraving published by the Savory Steam Press, Cirencester)

Kempsford Church.

wails alongside her watery grave to become one of the most enduring and oft-told ghost stories. Extracts are given here to summarise the scene that has changed but little over the centuries and the evergreen story.

> O'ertopt with waving weeds, or ivy green,
> With here and there a battlemented peak,
> That sadly shines among the glossy sheen,
> A long, low wall goes stretching, old and weak
> From orchard lawns there opes a rising way,
> With trees within and riverwards this wall,
> Which endeth in a room of ruins grey,
> Of shattered stones, and one grim window tall,
> And skeleton, when darkness lends her pall;
> The churchyard stones shine whitely thro' the trees,
> And life and death lie calm in sombre ease.

But ye, old stones, are singing now your songs.
A refrain of five hundred years ago,
The fog creeps up, and dimmer grows the moon;
The hazy, pliant imps grow less and less;
The harsh voiced music seeks a sweeter tune;
The spectres to the verge of darkness press,
And swiftly turn to elfin nothingness;
While, moving stately to her nightly tryst,
Appears the spirit 'Lady of the Mist'.

Upon a dripping fog-cloud, thick'ning still,
She stands bare-headed, and with naked feet,
Enwrapped in a mantle thin and chill,
And sleeveless arms upon her bosom meet,
Her face is white and cold, but clear and sweet;
Her eyes are softened stars divinely fair,
And meteor flashes move her auburn hair.

'Here I, poor Lady Maud, first woke to love,
My husband sought me in this ancient hall;
My Henry, rising high his peers above,
And jealous, lest this name ignobly fall,
Was honour's self, and noble all in all.
Days flew, until my husband, once unstrung,
Was caught up by a brother's older guile,
And in an evil hour his fortunes flung
In discontents and vain sedition's wile,
And rebel rising throughout Britain's isle.
And I was left to you, oh fields and streams,
To fearful fancies and disturbing dreams.

Then tidings reached me of a battle fought,
Which wrecked all future joy for me and mine;
And soon with us, king-hunted soldiers sought
Concealment from the axe or hempen line;

While oft we gave them hurried food and wine;
For to the beaten, sea coast seeking wight,
Our lane afforded ways for heedful flight.

One night my doors were barred, for driving rain,
With windy wailings made the meadows drear,
An urgent knocking called us up again;
A soldier entered, wary with his fear,
And standing in the gloom he called me near.
There, with his armour dimmed, and trampled crest,
My husband's brother craved both food and rest.

Unknown to all my servitors, he seemed
As some poor knight, who changeful fortune tries
Who journeys onward when the morning gleamed
And, well I ween, not one of them e'er deemed,
That thou receiv'st a guest, oh river room.
Him safely hiding in thy leafy gloom.

(At this stage Lady Maud's visits to the little river room, hidden among the trees by the water's edge, had been observed by a knight in her household whose advances she rejected. The knight took his revenge by getting a message to her husband telling him of Maud's clandestine meetings.)

Dark as his own black wraith he haunting came
And unseen, saw my nightly pilgrimage;
Then fled, his heart hot with unholy flame,
And turned my dear lord's love to burning rage.

My husband came, and lingered here unknown.
He sternly tracked my faint but guileless feet;
Saw falsely as he had been falsely shown,
And judged me rashly in his deep deceit

And madly rushed into the dark retreat,
Struck down his brother in the uncertain light,
And rudely snatched me to the pathway, white.

He caught me in his wrathful arms and threw
  Me shrieking, o'er the wall into the stream,
  Whose envious waters wildly rose and flew
Above my head, and all things seemed a dream,
    And life a far away, forgotten gleam,
  In darkness; then I felt, and shiv'ring stood
Among the weeds which swayed me from the flood.

  My husband saw his error, now too late;
Mourning his wife as one among the dead.
With mind distracted by his wretched fate,
He and his brother northward swiftly fled
Where rebel Barons hailed him as their head,
To curb the king by warlike word and deed
But fortune failed to help them in their need.
My husband lived to find his dull life yield
  The bitter harvest of a beggar's crust,
  To curse that night illusive, and his trust;
And then to see with disenchanted eyes
His faithful wife as from the grave arise.

And he who all our sorrow wrongly wrought
Whose hatred travelled further than he knew
  Was after haunted by regretful thought
  His fading years saw life with clearer view
And showed the pathway to the good and true.
The church received him, penitent, assoiled,
He lived a lowly monk, and prayed, and toiled.

Within in yon church's chancel he doth sleep
  Beneath a sculptured statue chill and pale

I watch his lonely spirit vigils keep
And see it shiver at my woeful wail.

Thus I, uneasy spirit, freedom crave,
For one hour's converse with the silent shades;
So nightly, granted victory o'er the grave,
I sing to charm old night 'til darkness fades,
And light darts silver on the grassy blades'

(The false knight, turned penitent monk, is another of the number of Kempsford's ghosts.)

AND THEREBY HANGS A TALE OF A HAUNTED HILL AND MACARONI

By June Lewis-Jones

The following tale is based on the Author's Notes prefacing the novel, The Witch's Mark *by June Lewis, published by Robert Hale Ltd in 1975. It is reproduced here by kind permission of the publishers.*

A local paper published a letter at the end of the Victorian period from a correspondent who had been shown the signs of an old dwelling house, known as Paul's Hill. A reply, the following week, bore out the information that Mrs E. Honour had given me: that a considerable house stood at one time on the spot known as Paul's Hill in the Leach Valley between Eastleach and Burford. Mrs Honour remembered passing the ruins of a large house with tall chimneys when she rode through that valley as a child.

Until recently a lone apple tree marked the spot where the house is reputed to have stood. Several field walls between Lappingwell and Sheepbridge have been built of squared stones, thought to be the remains of the house at Paul's Hill. These have now disappeared but George Swinford of Filkins recalled that as an apprentice mason he used a great deal of the stones from the derelict Paul's Hill house in what we know locally as Happy Valley to build Ravenshill at Eastleach Martin (the house is now known as Eastleach House and is famous for its beautiful gardens which are open to the public on specific dates during mid-summer). The ornate staircase is also said to have originally been the one from the house at Paul's Hill.

The parish registers for Eastleach Turville contain no reference to the name Paul. As a Christian name it only occurs twice, but in the register for Eastleach Martin, on 30 June 1547 a baptism is recorded of Johan, daughter of Richard Pulle. The writing is difficult to decipher and it could easily have been transcribed through the ages as Paul. It is not unreasonable to suppose that the house in question was named after its owner.

The lonely Leach Valley, leading to Macaroni Farm, in winter 1975

The two villages appear to have been united at one time in the fourteenth century and appear under the title of Leuge, or Long Turville; but subsequent records show the Eastleaches Turville and Martin running as separate parishes each with their respective church, separated by name and the river Leach but physically joined by a delightful clapper stone footbridge and an ancient stone build road bridge. From 6 March 1935, Turville and Martin (anciently and still locally known as Bouthrop) became officially one parish, served by one parish council under the simple title of Eastleach. Under any of its names, no parochial records throw up that of Paul's Hill, or Paul's Castle – as sometimes it has been referred to locally.

Likewise, to ascertain the truth that prevails on the naming of Macaroni Downs, which local lore would have us believe to have been the training ground of the Derby winner, Macaroni, the English Place Names Society records the name of Macaroni Farm for 1830, and it appears on property maps after that date – some considerable time before Macaroni won the Derby in 1863. It may be that the horse took its name from the valley in the Cotswolds, although it seems a little improbable as it was bred by the Marquis of Westminster at Eaton and it seems unlikely that Macaroni ever trod the turf of Macaroni Downs in Gloucestershire.

Macaroni, the Derby winner, does have a Christmas connection, albeit rather tenuously by name, as it was sired by Sweetmeat, who also sired Mincemeat and Mincepie – both winners in their time of the Oaks! Macaroni, as a place name, is most likely to have come from the time the Regency dandies frequented the old Bibury Races, sporting outrageously rakish hats atop equally outrageous hairstyles, to become known as the Macaroni set and satirised in the song about 'sticking a feather in his hat and called him Macaroni'. The old Bibury Race meeting had its peregrinations taken from Upton Down at Burford, where it was founded in 1681 as an outcome of a visit by Charles II to Nell Gwynne at Burford Priory (*cherchez la femme*) and did a lot of travelling in the Cotswolds before going to Wiltshire. In 1899, the club took over the Salisbury racecourse.

The mysterious house at Paul's Hill (sketch by courtesy of Robert Hale,
publishers of *The Witch's Mark*)

To return to the mystery of the history of Paul's Hill, is to site the house on the route along the Leach Valley to the uplands where the old race course once resounded to the thundering hooves of the horses and the fields echoed with the cacophony of riders and race-goers, where peer and peasant, pedlar and pick-pocket jostled with the rich and reckless and riff-raff in a great social circle around the Cotswold races.

To add to the mystery and romance of Pauls' Hill is that local legend has it that on Christmas Eve, if the moon is full, on the stroke of midnight the house appears, lights blazing, a ball is in full progress. A coach and horses are heard coming out of the dark valley towards the house. A shot is fired. And the scene vanishes.

THE MISTLETOE BOUGH

Written by Nathaniel Thomas Haynes Bayly (1797-1839)

This poem by one of the most prolific authors of dramatic works, songs, stories and stage plays, all written at great speed – of which Perfection *was acclaimed as the most successful – tells the tragic tale of a young bride of one of the Lords Lovell who met her untimely end while playing hide and seek during the wedding festivities one Christmastide at the family home at Minster Lovell Hall. Although a number of Bayly's verses had been held up to ridicule, this story is based on a tragedy that was brought to light explaining the mystery of the bride who vanished. An earlier tragedy had been discovered when, in 1708, an, 'entire skeleton of a man, as having been sitting at a table, which was before him, with a book, paper, pen, etc, etc; in another part of the room lay a cap; all much mouldred and decayed. Which the family and others judged to be this Lord Lovell, whose exit hath hitherto been so uncertain'. The report of this find was written by William Cowper, clerk of the*

Parliament, to Francis Peck, in his day a reputable antiquary, during work on the hall when a secret chamber was discovered. The Lord Lovell, whose remains it was thought to be, had disappeared after his escape from the battle of Stoke in 1487. Legend has it that Lovell sought refuge in the old family home at Minster Lovell and was hidden in a secret room by a trusty servant; the circumstances under which the fugitive was left, locked and sealed in the room to die of starvation, are the mystery. Likewise, which of the succeeding Lords Lovell lost his bride on their wedding night, as dramatised by Bayly in this poem, is not made clear.

Minster Lovell church as seen from the ruined Minster Hall, scene of a Christmastide tragedy

The mistletoe hung in the castle hall,
The holly branch shone on the old oak wall;
And the baron's retainers were blithe and gay,
And keeping their Christmas holiday.
The baron beheld with a father's pride
His beautiful child, young Lovell's bride;
While she with her bright eyes seem'd to be
The star of the goodly company.

'I'm weary of dancing now;' she cried;
'Here tarry a moment – I'll hide – I'll hide!
And, Lovell, be sure thou'rt first to trace
The clue to my secret lurking place.'
Away she ran – and her friends began
Each tower to search, and each nook to scan;
And young Lovell cried, 'Oh where dost thou hide?
I'm lonesome without thee, my own dear bride.'

They sought her that night! And they sought her next day!
And they sought her in vain when a week pass'd away!
In the highest – and lowest – the loneliest spot,
Young Lovell sought wildly – but found her not.
And years flew by, and their grief at last
Was told as a sorrowful tale long past;
And when Lovell appeared, the children cried,
'See! The old man weeps for his fairy bride.'

At length an oak chest, that had long lain hid,
Was found in the castle – they raised the lid –
And a skeleton form lay mouldering there,
In the bridal wreath of that lady fair!
Oh! sad was her fate! – in sportive jest
She hid from her lord in the old oak chest.
It closed with a spring! – and a dreadful doom,
The bride lay clasp'd in her living tomb!

DICK WHITTINGTON
FACTS AND FABLE

By Hope Costley White

The following summary from Mrs Costley White's story of one of Gloucestershire's most famous sons, published in her book, Gloucestershire Stories, *in 1949 by The British Publishing Company of Gloucester, which she based on extensive research, shows that the facts of Dick Whittington's life are no less interesting than the fictionalised fable. In his Foreword to her book, Lawrence Tanner, Keeper of the Muniments and Library of Westminster Abbey, paid tribute to the author's, 'refusal to put the famous cat back into the legendary bag. The pedants have tried to kill and commercialise poor puss – not even "felix ... opportunitate mortis," – by telling us that the word is merely a corruption of the French word* achat *but here we find evidence produced to show that a cat, a real English cat, was confidently associated with Whittington within a few years of his death'.*

Richard Whittington was born in 1358, the youngest son of Sir William Whittington, in the manor house close to the old Norman church in Pauntley in Gloucestershire. He was only two years old when his father died and, no doubt, despite being of a landowning family, Richard's widowed mother would have found some difficulty in launching her three sons. At the age of thirteen, Richard was sent to London to become an apprentice to Sir John Fitzwarren, a mercer and merchant adventurer, himself a West Country man and a friend of the family. Sir John was a great city merchant and the young Richard Whittington was fascinated by the pageantry of his master's liveried company of the Mercers, the busy city life and the seafaring craft and folk of the merchant adventurers whom he met in the Pool of London.

By the age of thirty-five, Richard Whittington had become a successful merchant himself, with five apprentices bound to him, and elected alderman of Broad Street, serving as Sheriff in 1393-1394 having, by then, married his master's daughter, Alice. His career leapt forward in legendary steps, and he was lending money to the Crown by 1400. The triumph of Agincourt was, it is said, due in no small measure to Whittington, who had advanced large sums of money to Henry V. The King offered repayment of the loan at a celebratory banquet after the victorious battle. Richard took the bonds from the King and threw them into the fire. 'Never had prince such a subject,' said the King. 'Never had subject such a prince,' replied Whittington. One of the lights in the easternmost window in Westminster Abbey perpetuates the royal connection: Henry V is shown in full armour alongside a statuette of Richard Whittington with his cat.

Richard Whittington, from an engraving by John Elstrach, 1590, used as the frontispiece of Samuel Lyson's book, *The Model Merchant of the Middle Ages*

True to the nursery rhyme, Whittington was at least thrice Mayor of London. His wise leadership of the city earned him the respect of his contemporaries and his public-spirited benefactions included bringing water by way of leaden pipes to the citizens of London, founding the library of the Grey Friars in Newgate Street, repairing the Hospital of St Bartholomew, extensively improving the conditions in Newgate Gaol, and re-building a church at Paternoster Lane at his own expense. Richard Whittington died in 1423, after his wife, Alice. They had no children and his great wealth was distributed between various institutions for the benefit of church and community.

The association with the famous cat has been attributed to a number of sources: it would not have been unusual for Richard Whittington to have had a cat as a pet, cats had been valued as excellent mouse-hunters and loyal friends throughout many cultures; a painting of Richard Whittington, dated 1560, which once hung in the Mercers' Hall, shows him with a cat, as does an engraving by John Elstrach, dated 1590, which forms the frontispiece of Samuel Lysons' book, *The Model Merchant of the Middle Ages*. But it is back in the county of his birth, that the tradition of Whittington and his cat has an early connection. During repairs in 1862 of a house in St Mary's Street, documented as 'the tenement of Richard Whittington', a figure of a boy with a cat in his arms was found on a broken stone in the cellar. It would appear that the immediate relatives knew of the cat legend and were content to perpetuate the story. Back to London, though: the mummified body of a cat preserved in the Natural History Museum is said to have been found in a corner, near the tower, of St Michael's church where Richard Whittington was buried.

DICK WHITTINGTON – BUT WHAT ABOUT THE PANTOMIME

Staged at the Everyman Theatre

In the sixteenth century, Dick's tale was completely changed as his financial successes were attributed to the help of his cat! In a play of 1606, three of the elements we see today are mentioned: the cat, Dick's early poverty and his eventual knighthood. Six years later a ballad provides the rest of the picture: Dick's employment by a city merchant, his work as a scullion, his flight to the country, the prophecy of the bells, the loan of the cat, the cat's destruction of rats in a far off land, the gratitude of the ruler, Dick's return with a ship full of gold, his rise to fame, his service three times as mayor and the burning of King Henry's bonds.

It was in pantomime that the myth of Dick Whittington grew. As the nineteenth century progressed, other characters such as Idle Jack and King Rat joined the story. Dick was normally played by a girl and the Fitzwarren's cook was played by a man.

Productions became increasingly magnificent with songs, routines and dances influenced by music hall. Most of these were quite irrelevant to the plot! In one production, Augustus Harris and Arthur Collins, successively managers at Drury Lane, engaged hundreds of actors, changing into thousands of costumes.

Dick Whittington, the folk hero of pantomime (poster by courtesy of the Everyman Theatre, Cheltenham)

Dick Whittington and Panto Cat inside the Everyman Theatre (photo: Rob Lacey, courtesy of the Everyman Theatre, Cheltenham)

A few behind-the-scenes facts of the Everyman Theatre production, Christmas 2003

+ The costumes for the pantomime took ten people eight weeks to make. Every costume was made specifically for the actor to ensure a perfect fit.
+ The cast rehearsed for approximately 140 hours.
+ Sarah Suet, the cook, had more costume changes than any other character, seven in total, every one with a different wig.
+ At his widest point, Graham the octopus measured eight metres.
+ Six people were involved in painting the set: each front measured ten metres long by five metres high. It took two painters working

full-time over nine days to paint each one, which folded small
enough to fit into a suitcase.

+ The cast doesn't get to rehearse on stage, with the set, until three
  days before the pantomime opens.

+ Writer and director, Sue Colverd, began writing the panto in
  February, just one month after the end of the previous year's
  pantomime.

+ The set for Dick Whittington was twice as large as the previous
  pantomimes, and the number of costumes was increased by
  seventy-five per cent.

+ Some 115 schools from as far away as Hereford and Monmouthsire
  went to see Dick Whittington: the total was an all time record!

*New Year and
Winters Past*

ANNO DOMINI

From 'Focal Point', published in the East Cotswold Church Monthly, *December 1968*

Anno Domini (the year of the Lord) is so familiar an expression that we easily overlook the miracle it represents. This is the miracle: that many millions of people throughout the generations have assented to the judgment that when Jesus was born a new world came to birth also.

On the day of the nativity of Jesus, the wildest imagination could not have conceived of such a possibility. Every factor of geography, history, religion and politics was against it.

Yet 500 years later, the world was ready to divide all history into two parts: Before Christ (BC) and In the year of the Lord (*Anno Domini* – AD). Many efforts have been made to number the years from what were held to be notable events. Creation (Genesis) was the starting point of Jewish reckoning and indeed still is. According to the Jewish calendar Jesus was born in 3165 or 3166 *Anno Mondi* (AM).

The Romans first reckoned years from the founding of Rome (about 750 years before the birth of Jesus) but were doing so from accession of Diocletian (284 AD) when the *Anno Domini* system superseded it.

Just to complete the story, it was a Scythian monk, Dionysius, who was given the job of working out the years in AD terms. Expert in chronology, as he was, we know now he was something like six years out in his reckoning of the first Christmas.

Winter as depicted in a mosaic pavement at Chedworth Roman Villa

New Year's Day

By the Rt Revd Bishop of Derry and Raphoe, published by The Religious Tract Society in The Sunday at Home Annual 1905–06

The significance of New Year's Day is like the significance of a milestone. The milestone does not reckon accurate distances from my hall-door, nor make any allowance for my divergences from the road. Yet the recurrence of one milestone after another helps me to measure, roughly though it be, alike my distance and my speed. There is no magic in the measurement; in a foreign country kilometres answer just as well.

Vale View homestead at snowbound Minchinhampton (Photo: Katie Jarvis)

And so New Year's Day is an arbitrary institution. If we had chosen instead to observe the first of February or of December, that date would have come to us with all the significance which now the first of January claims, and with as much or as little reason.

In truth, we suffer at times some small inconvenience from the fact that our calendar has actually been shifted – from the differences between the old style and the new, between the Russian calendar and our own.

From any given date to the same in the next year, we have closed a circle around the sun, and begun another, quite as perfect as that from one New Year's Day to the next. Neither one nor other is a perfect circle at all, or else, what is the meaning of the extra day in leap year?

Note: It is interesting that a century later – in 2005-2006 a 'leap second' was made to compensate for the earth slowing down

GLOUCESTERSHIRE WASSAIL

Traditional

Wassail, Wassail, all over the town
Our toast it is white, and our ale it is brown
Our bowl it is made of the white maple tree
With the wassailing bowl we'll drink to thee
So here is to Cherry and to his right cheek
Pray God send our master a good piece of beef
And a good piece of beef that we may all see
With the wassailing bowl we'll drink to thee
And here is to Dobbin and to his right eye

Pray God send our master a good Christmas pie
And a good Christmas pie that we may all see
With our wassailing bowl we'll drink to thee
So here is to Broad May and to her broad horn
May God send our master a good crop of corn
And a good crop of corn that we may all see
With the wassailing bowl we'll drink to thee
And here is to Fillpail and to her left ear
Pray God send our master a happy New Year
And a happy New Year as e'er he did see
With our wassailing bowl we'll drink to thee
And here is to Colly and to her long tail
Pray God send our master he never may fail
A bowl of strong beer, I pray you draw near
And our jolly wassail it's then you shall hear

Wassailing the apple trees is an ancient ritual still carried out in odd corners of
the Cotswolds and the West Country

Come butler, come fill us a bowl of the best
Then we hope that your soul in heaven may rest
But if you do draw us a bowl of the small
Then down shall go butler, bowl and all

Then here's to the maid in the lily white smock
Who tripped to the door and slipped back the lock
Who tripped to the door and pulled back the pin
For to let these jolly wassailers in.

CHRISTMAS PARTIES AT COWBRIDGE

By Bob Browning

Tracing the history of Cowbridge estate on the edge of the ancient town of Malmesbury, and the grand country house that was to be central to the EKCO factory where radar was researched and developed during the Second World War, Bob Browning paints an evocative picture of works parties in the lean post-war period in his book, EKCO's of Cowbridge, House and War Factory. *In its time, the radio and electronics factory employed hundreds of workers from the South Cotswold area and had outworkers at the Polish camp at Daglingworth. This extract is reproduced by kind permission of the author, Bob Browning, and publisher, Cowbridge Publishing, Malmesbury.*

The highlight of the year for many people was the Christmas parties – and the children's Christmas party is remembered by just about everyone who attended it. Somewhat oddly this event always took place early in January.

The children's party started in the 1950s when food rationing was still in force. Originally for children of the staff, the party soon grew to accommodate all the children in town. David Forward remembers with great affection waiting for the party invitations to arrive. These were not sent to the parents of the children. Each individual child had his or her invitation brought to its door, by the postman. David describes the cards as being special, being coloured and having scalloped edges.

Parents were issued with labels to attach to their offspring. They were told at what time the coach would collect the children, also the time they would be returned. On arrival the label was torn into three; one part stayed with the child; one went with his or her coat to a specific cloakroom and the third part was given to a coach steward. Everything went like a military operation. A coach took children up to the age of thirteen to the factory canteen, which was unrecognisable. The walls had been covered with Disney characters, all hand drawn and painted by Ken Gough from Hullavington who worked as an electrician at Cowbridge. Each figure was just the size of a child.

Children's party at EKCO, Cowbridge

Decorations hung from the ceiling and there were balloons everywhere. The stage had been converted into a living room complete with fireplace and this too had been decorated for Christmas. The children were fed jellies and ice cream, and tinned fruit; a rare treat in those austere times. After this it was time for games followed by a film show of cartoons, something, again, which at that time was almost unknown to the vast majority of children. This was long before every household had television and a trip to the local cinema was a special occasion. There were stage acts and clowns – all put on by the factory staff. The highlight was of course Father Christmas's arrival, heralded by a bell being rung very loudly in another room. All the children had been gathered together and were then told 'Father Christmas has just come through Brinkworth'. The children were then told to shout very loudly so that HE would know where to turn off the main road. They were then told it was not loud enough and he had passed on through to Sherston. After a few 'diversion' like this, the noise generated was similar to a Beatles concert! Imagine the excitement of 400 or so children as they eventually saw Father Christmas arrive. All eyes were on the stage to watch a sledge actually come through the fireplace.

Tom Stevens had arrived at Cowbridge as a very young man and had guarded the house prior to Sir Philip Hunloke's arrival with his family. Tom stayed on to work for EKCO and is remembered as Father Christmas by literally hundreds of Malmesbury people. Throughout the year he would pay visits to Swindon Market to buy presents, bring them home and wrap them ready for distribution at the Children's party. His own two young children were totally unaware of his double identity so this he could only do after they had gone to bed! During the party the stage and sledge were prepared and the window at the back of the living room had snow falling behind it! This was managed by simply putting a fan inside some shuttering behind the window then feeding the fan with small pieces of torn up white tissue paper.

Tom's daughter Val went to the party along with all her friends and used to go up and receive her present with them – blissfully unaware of her father's double life! As well as the huge cotton wool beard and disguised voice, Tom always wore calfskin gauntlet gloves to help hide his identity. One Christmas he had mislaid the gloves and had to appear without them. When it was his daughter's turn to receive her present she sat on Father Christmas's lap, and looked down to discover she was looking at her own father's hands. All her dreams were shattered and she burst into tears. Father Christmas was not real!

New Year Needles and Threads Custom

Queen's College, Oxford

With grateful acknowledgment for permission to use this information from the Keeper of the Archives at Queen's College, Oxford University.

Queen's College is named after Queen Philippa, wife of Edward III, and holds faith with an ancient and unique custom at New Year, known as the needles and threads ceremony. Derived from a play on the founder's name, Eglesfield, which translates into *Aiguilles et fils*, the needles and threads are distributed by the Bursar following the New Year dinner. The needles are threaded with black, blue and red silk. The first are given to the Theologians, the second to Legists and Medical Graduates, and the third to Artists. As each needle is handed over, the Bursar bids the recipient to 'Take this and be thrifty'.

Whoops! Hector Jones has a slip-up to the delight of his children, Heather and Ralph (Photo: courtesy Lilian Jones)

The Promenade, Cheltenham, probably 1920s (Photo: Cheltenham Newspapers)

WINTERS PAST

'We don't get winters like we used to have in the old days' has been a
stock phrase for generations by older generations – a random garnering
of reports of winters past certainly throws up some spectacular records.

250 AD	The Thames froze for 9 weeks
695	The Thames froze for 6 weeks and booths were built on it
923	The Thames froze for 13 weeks
1035	Severe frost on 24th June: corn and fruit destroyed
1063	The Thames froze for 14 weeks
1076	'A dreadful frost' continued from November until April
1114	Several wooden bridges were carried away by ice
1407	Frost lasted for 15 weeks, all (?) small birds perished
1434	The Thames was frozen down as far as Gravesend
1607	Thames frozen enough for fires and 'diversions' to be held on it
1683	Frost lasted 13 weeks. Forest trees and even the sturdy oaks of England were split by frost. Most of the holly trees were killed. Ice 11 inches thick reported on the Thames
1716	Fair held on the ice on the Thames and oxen roasted. Frost lasted from 24th November until 9th February
1739	Frost for 9 weeks. Coaches 'plied on the ice on the Thames'. It was described as 'a hard winter'.
1814	Booths again erected on the frozen Thames
1844–45	The frost on Good Friday (21st March) was so severe that canal boats were unable to travel

1879   Recalled as The Wet Summer, spoken of in terms of awesome respect and terror as The Great War as a benchmark of 'bad weather', and 'Seventy-Nine' passed into weather lore when skating began in the Cotswolds a week before Christmas and winter continued into May, as this poem (published in the *Wilts and Gloucestershire Standard* at the time) shows.

Landgirls enjoying the snow of 1940 (Photo: Joyce Large)

The Merry Month of May, 1879

Put on your warmest things
Draw closer round the fire
And though it's still at 23
Let's pile the Silkstone higher
Let us be merry – though we are
From going out debarred
For 'tis the genial month of May
And look! It's snowing hard

A footnote to one of the articles in the same paper warned its readers: 'it would be a little short of madness to buy railway shares or have one's hair cut.'

The age-old simile 'as slow a-coming as Cotswold barley' could never have been more apt than in that year, for the crops on the Cotswolds were not brought in until New Year's Day of 1880, with frost on the barley ails as another winter started.

BRITAIN BATTLES WITH THE WEATHER
1939-40

By Elizabeth Speller

This extract from Elizabeth Speller's highly acclaimed book, The Sunlight on the Garden: a family in love, war and madness, *published by Granta (2006), opens the chapter on the early part of the Second World War with an evocative pen portrait of the 1939-40 winter in the Cotswolds. It* is reproduced here by kind permission of Elizabeth Speller and the publishers.

Hamlet: Goes it against the main of Poland, sir, Or for some frontier?
Captain: Truly to speak, and with no addition,
We go to gain a little patch of ground
That hath no profit in it but the name
(Hamlet, Act IV)

Britain battles with the weather rather than the Germans in the winter months of 1939-40. Blizzards immobilize the whole country. The temperature continues to fall after Christmas and record figures of more than 20 degrees below freezing are recorded in the last week of January. An ice storm shrouds the west; the Mersey, Humber and Severn freeze over and the Grand Union Canal is solid all the way from Birmingham to London. The sea freezes at Bognor, the harbour mouths at Southampton and Folkestone are impassable and the Thames turns to ice for eight miles between Teddington and Sunbury.

At the Round House, Lechlade, the whole world is white and still. Frost glazes the inside of the windows and, outside, the Thames, almost at its source, is motionless under the crystallised branches of overhanging willows. The burden of ice causes telegraph wires to snap and birds, unable to fly, die in the hedgerows. Beyond the river snow-covered pasture fades into a misty horizon and when the sun sets the fields, river and sky are lit with a fire that is without heat.

The Ice Storm of 1940

Robert Peel wrote of the phenomena of the ice storm that happened during the week-end of 27 January, 1940, published in the now extinct The Gloucestershire Countryside *magazine in the April 1940 issue. It has not been possible to trace the author of this feature, extracts of which are given below and although the period follows Christmastide, outstanding winters of the past still hold a fascination to us and bear out the oft-quoted saying that 'winters aren't like they used to be'. Robert Peel explains how this particular phenomena happened, producing some spectacular scenes.*

Occurring in the middle of a period of the greatest frost for over forty years, the storm was preceded by a period of comparative thaw when the temperature rose above freezing. By the evening of January 27th however the temperature fell to about 31 degrees F and a very fine rain began, almost a mist, which froze immediately as it settled. CJP Case, Esq, Past President of the RMS, in his explanation of the storm in *The Times* suggested that this rain as it fell became 'under cooled' or slightly below freezing point but remained liquid until the impact with exposed objects made it freeze. Polar explorers have reported cases where the sea in conditions of great calm has, as it were, hesitated to freeze in spite of its temperature going slightly below freezing point, but the disturbance caused by a pebble being thrown in has caused it to freeze over instantly.

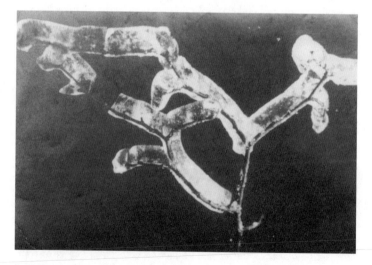

Ice 2½in-thick encasing a twig during the ice storm of 1940 (Photo: meteorological staff during their time at Wycliffe College, Stonehouse)

The rain continued to fall and freeze, coating the trees, telegraph wires and grass with crystal-clear ice. The wind rose to force 4 and 5 and it was soon apparent that the deposit of ice was increasing faster on the windward side. Grass and mere twigs became encased in ice one inch in diameter. Telegraph wires became long ropes of clear ice and were estimated to be carrying 80 to 90 lbs on each wire between the poles. A twig about one-eighth of an inch in diameter weighed with and without ice was found to be carrying twenty-eight times its own weight. It should occasion no surprise that branches burst, blocking roads, and telegraph wires and poles were brought down in great numbers. The coating of ice robbed tree branches of their natural flexibility, making them much more liable to snap as the rising wind made them groan and rattle together like bags of bones. Reports were made that even birds had, in these conditions, become frozen to branches as they perched, but so far as is known this was not seen in Gloucestershire.

The might of the Severn Bore lifted the ice on the river creating this scene more reminiscent of the Antarctic than Gloucestershire in 1940 (Photo: *Gloucester Journal*)

PC Hector Evans patrolled on his bike to the boundary of his beat at the middle of the frozen Severn in 1940 (Photo: *Gloucester Journal*)

The ice remained on the trees, etc for two or three days, when a slight thaw allowed the ice to melt, but it was interesting to note the ice fell off as if the twigs and wires carrying it became warmer inside first.

The conditions required to permit such a storm to take place – a warm belt of air carrying rain, the cold atmosphere through which it fell and the exposed surfaces at the right temperature to cause the ice to adhere – are happily rare in coinciding, but no one who witnessed this interesting phenomena will forget it.

Photographs of the most remarkable winter scenes ever recorded in Gloucestershire show the frozen Severn in the early days of February after the high tide had broken up the ice. It is over sixty years scenes such as these were last observed in Gloucestershire. Not only did they reveal extraordinary devastation, but no one will forget the sight of the ice-covered fields and commons resembling rough, pebbly beaches or the beauty of sunlight through the ice-bound tracery of bushes and trees. Overnight the whole landscape became transformed into deepest winter, and we know that the traditional savage winters of earlier days are in no way an exaggeration as many of us have believed until this year.

Testing the Waters

The following two memories of cycling and walking on the Thames at Lechlade in 1963 were first recorded by June Lewis-Jones for her book Fairford and Lechlade, *in the Oral History Series, published by Tempus Publishing Ltd in 2001 and reproduced here by permission of the author and publisher.*

CYCLING ON THE THAMES

We had always heard about the Big Freeze when it was said there was an ox roast on the Thames, but that was a couple of hundred years ago – in the history books. I never expected anything like that sort of winter in my lifetime, but I heard that the Thames was frozen right over, so I went off on my bike to see. Well, I saw our local policeman walk across from one bank to the other; he was a big fellow and someone told me he weighed eighteen stone, so I thought that if the ice took his weight I would try it on my bike. I was amazed how smooth it was to ride on the iced-up river, I didn't wobble at all and carried on right down the middle of the river, under the Ha'penny Pike Bridge and through the other side; then there was a great splintering noise and the ice cracked right across just a few yards behind me – that made me wobble a bit, especially as I thought at that moment, 'Help, I can't swim'. By then there was quite a gathering of people on the banks; I remember Mrs Titchener – Bert's wife – she was absolutely flabbergasted that I was riding on the river and took several photos. Then a few more people joined in, one or two more on bikes, others slipping and sliding about and – a couple on proper ice-skates – but further upriver from where I had just come from.

The next day the ice was under water. Only a few months ago a little group of children was coming from the school and they pointed to me and shouted out: 'there he is, there's the man that rode his bike on the river'. I asked them how they knew about it, it was so long ago and they said they had been told about it in their local history lesson: I never thought I would be known to be part of Lechlade history.

Jim Luce

Jim Luce cycling on frozen Thames at Lechlade

NO SLIP UP

On the historic day when the Thames was frozen enough for us to walk across, I joined in although I was pregnant with our youngest son, John, at the time. It was a bit precarious. Although, as a doctor, I knew what to do if he decided to come earlier than expected. But I did make the return trip a bit quicker because I did not want him born 'on the other side' as the middle of the river is the county border between Wiltshire and Gloucestershire. But all was well and he is Gloucestershire-born, so all county honour preserved!

Dr Sheila Stephens

The Year of the Pigeons

By John Moore

The following extract is from John Moore's book, The Year of the Pigeons, *published by Collins in 1963, and reproduced here by generous permission of The John Moore Society.*

We missed a white Christmas by a few hours; the first snow fell on Boxing Day. Its coming somewhat pacified those gloomy old men in the pub who are always complaining at this time of year that winters aren't what they used to be. One old gaffer holds that none of our weather is quite what it used to be, for which he blames, not the atom-bombs, but "summer-time", mucking about with the calendar, interfering with God's time (by which I suppose he means GMT). In 1752, when Parliament "mucked about with the calendar" in a big way, people like him caused riots in the streets. In order to correct an accumulated error caused by the old, inaccurate "Julian calendar", Parliament had passed an Act to the effect that in 1752 "11 days should be omitted, after September 2nd, so that the ensuing day should be September 14th." Simple folk believed that their rulers, whom they had no special reason to trust, were somehow defrauding them out of a slice of precious time: 11 whole day, one thirty-third of a year, a two-thousandth fraction of a man's allotted span! Rather pathetically, the poor people to whom time meant chief labour and squalor and hunger came out in the streets of London and marched about there, yelling: "Give us back our eleven days!"

The old men sniffed the air and began to tell us that there was "summat in the wind".

"As the days lengthen, the cold strengthens," they told us with grim satisfaction.

One evening, about a week after Christmas, we all became aware of "something coming" suddenly. There was a distinct, but indefinable change in the quality of the cold. You couldn't easily explain it. You could say that the difference between today's wind and yesterday's was like the difference between steel and iron. I was reminded of the cold "like something sentient" which "came out of the east, striding", in Belloc's marvellous description of Napolean's retreat from Moscow. During the night of December 30th the cold strode across Gloucestershire. We heard the wind of its passing as we lay in bed; turned over and went to sleep again, with that Siberian wolf-howl still in our ears. In the morning, aware of some strangeness, we got up and ran to the window. At first there was nothing to be seen but the blurred grey-white of thick snow blown horizontally. When our eyes got used to the phenomenon dim shapes loomed up: outbuildings, the gate into the paddock, the forms of animals rather like pictures on the walls of a prehistoric cave, animals seen dimly before dawn. These turned out to be the three horses which live out, encrusted with snow, standing beside the gate.

We were snowed in, and the whole village was snowed in, individually and collectively. A man could dig his way down his garden path into the lane; and he could make his way along the lane until he came to the village street; and there was the pub, and the village store. All the roads out of the village were blocked; we were quite shut in, a situation rather rare in England, we were a community on its own.

It was fun at first. Humans are adaptable creatures. A few people discovered skis in attics, relics of old Swiss holidays, and remembered how to use them. At least a score of toboggans were routed out by the children. I rode Zena through the soft snow, which came up to her knees; I felt her quivering with excitement, anxiety, near-panic, but had the comfortable certainty that if she really panicked and tried to gallop away I had only to pull her into the nearest snowdrift to stop her dead.

John Moore with Zena (Photo: courtesy of The John Moore Society)

Then the wind howled louder, and the snow froze hard. And I couldn't ride her out of the drive, let alone down the lane for exercise.

NEVER MISSED AN EDITION EVEN IN
WINTER 1962-63

By Ted Hughes

The Wilts and Gloucestershire Standard, *which has served the Cotswolds since 1837, published a souvenir issue in 1987 to mark its 150th anniversary and Ted Hughes, the advertising manager, wrote of the mammoth task of getting the newspaper through to the towns and villages during the longest snowbound period in living memory.*

Locally and affectionately the Wilts and Gloucestershire Standard *is still referred to as* The Hedger and Ditcher *– from the days when the front page was entirely filled with columns of advertisements (in the style of* The Times *of old). But in this agricultural area the situations vacant and wanted and sales of implements and property were all related to farm work and workers and domestic service.*

The first edition was published as a four-page paper with an opening column giving a dignified announcement to, 'the Nobility, Gentry and Clergy and inhabitants, generally of the Counties of Wilts and Gloucester'. The distinctive gabled front of the office in Dyer Street at Cirencester still bears the word 'Printers' over the door – a remnant of the days when the paper was printed on site. In the early days customers were invited to watch the printing by steam using a cylinder machine.

The following extract of how the news got through in the hazardous conditions of 1962-63 is reproduced here by kind permission of the Editor, Wilts and Gloucestershire Standard.

Snow drifts at Ampney St Peter, 1963 (Photo: *Wilts and Gloucestershire Standard*)

It is our proud claim that the Standard has not missed an edition in the whole 150 years since publication first started, but we came close to missing several editions in the winter of 1962-63. On the evening of Boxing Day, heavy falls of snow started, and it was not until February that we were to see the ground again. Many villages were totally cut off from Cirencester for weeks, and indeed Cirencester itself was isolated on the last weekend of 1962. The roads were cleared after Herculean efforts by all concerned by the Monday, whereupon a further blizzard and gale force winds cut the town off on 2 January 1963.

The Market Place, Cirencester 1963 (Photo: *Wilts and Gloucestershire Standard*)

Drifts of snow as much as six feet high were recorded in many places, the local policeman at Daglingworth made efforts to get into Cirencester for bread for the village, and life was a battle for survival for many weeks. In those days, *the Standard* was printed late on Thursday evenings at Dursley, and deliveries made, as now, direct to towns and villages throughout the area as soon as the papers were off the press.

That weekend, the route to and from Dursley, via Tetbury and Calcot crossroads, was entirely blocked, so arrangements were made to take the papers by road via Cam to Stroud railway station. They were then loaded on to the Kemble train on Friday morning, and collected from there by a fleet of vans and private cars for distribution.

Two people were assigned to each delivery vehicle, armed with shovels and Wellingtons. I well remember walking through snowdrifts up to my waist, with two bundles of papers on my shoulders, and finally arriving at the home of Mr Taylor of Coates. I was the first person from outside the village to get through, and was rewarded with a welcome glass of sherry.

In 1963, there was still a printing operation at Cirencester, under the redoubtable Ted Maslin. Sales particulars were printed for among others, Hobbs and Chambers; a monthly newspaper for the Americans at Fairford; plus many items for local firms and organisations. Many of the articles for *The Standard,* and the classified advertisements, were set at Cirencester. All this used a lot of hot metal which was brought daily from Dursley. A number of Cirencester people worked at the Dursley printing works and took with them each morning the articles already set in type, and returned each evening with bars of solid metal for use by their colleagues at Cirencester. This was an excellent arrangement until the weather turned against us. We eventually ended up with masses of articles at Cirencester, but no metal, while Dursley had plenty of metal but no stories!

We knew that the roads were almost impassable, but with a double shift of men waiting to work at Cirencester with no materials, I volunteered to try to get through. With a Dormobile loaded with type, and Charlie Payne riding shotgun, we set off for Tetbury but were told by the police there that a single lane had been cut through to Beverstone, but warned us that if we got stuck or if we met something coming the other way it would be at our own risk as there were no rescue facilities. We drove on and slid and slithered past Beverstone eventually deciding to risk the longer route through Nailsworth. I have never done the Cresta Run, but now have an idea how it feels after traversing the hill down into Nailsworth at high speed, turning the steering wheel from lock to lock in my efforts to keep on course.

My co-driver's expression is etched on my memory to this day. He was gripping the dashboard, white-knuckled, his face as white as the snow which shot past him just outside the van, with a look of utter terror! We were greeted at Dursley like men from outer space, and after changing over our loads, made our tortuous way back to Cirencester, relieved that the county council snow plough had forced a better passage up Nailsworth hill.

Later that month one driver managed to drive down into Compton Abdale and drop his bundle of papers for the village, but could not climb the hill again. He tried for almost an hour, but finally gave up and returned to the village. He untied some bundles of the papers, wrapped himself in them, and spent the night in the van in extremely cold temperatures. At first light he started the van and drove the whole way up the hill with no problem at all. He later told us that he did not know whether to laugh or cry. Despite all these problems we were able to get the newspapers out each week, if rather later than we should have liked, and we can still say that in spite of two world wars and adverse weather conditions etc *the Standard* has not missed an edition in its first 150 years – let us hope we can keep that record for the next 150!

THE ROUND HOUSE, INGLESHAM

By Elizabeth Speller

*The regional first prize winner in the Faber/Ottakers Poetry Competition 2003,
this poem draws on the author's vivid memories of being marooned in the Round
House when the upper reaches of the Thames were under winter floods, and is
reproduced here by kind permission of Elizabeth Speller.*

That winter we ran aground. Water
stretched as far as Lechlade spire, sucked thick round squat willows, silenced
the lock gates,
where the old bridge arched from its bed and poles, still rigged, whispered of
roads lying low beneath the flood.
While somewhere in the moving flat between us and the rest of the world the
river scoured and tugged.
Indivisible.
We laid fortifications: sacks of sand along each small, overlooked place which
might be considered an entrance.
Caulked house and thoughts against the mud and the mess and the dark.
But the river lapped and coiled and called in the night and our breath
betrayed us, running down the glass.
Hazed with burning oil, the house ached damp in its bones;
Dogs pee'd on the floor, the baby coughed, and the water rose-
moulds clustering in the flutes of curtains, spore-bursts smudged across a wall-
rose and kept us at bay, small before the fire,

rose from underneath, up the lime bank with the smell of old, sedulous water,
beading the stone skin, slippery with sweat.
No sailor attempting the measure of a flat world,
was more lonely than my father, toiling our slight boat in absent fields
letting the current find him,
trusting that some watery fortune would see him sound.

Flooded fields from Inglesham to Lechlade, viewed from the Round House
(Photo: Elizabeth Speller)

A COUNTRYWOMAN'S NOTES

By Rosemary Verey

Evoking the sights and smells of the Cotswold countryside in which she created the famous Barnsley House gardens at her family home, the late Rosemary Verey became a legend in her own lifetime, outstanding among the great gardening greats whose names are as familiar as those of the humble hedgerow flowers and trees in a meadow of which she wrote with as much affection and knowledge as the breathtaking planting schemes in her award-winning garden. In his 'Foreword' to A Countrywoman's Notes, *from which these extracts are taken, Prince Charles, a Cotswold neighbour, fellow gardener and enthusiast for country ways, described the publication, printed by Rosemary Verey's daughter, Davina Wynne-Jones, on her private press, Gryffon Publications, as a 'beautiful book'. It is.*

Following in the Arts and Crafts tradition that centred on the Cotswolds a crow's flight away from Kelmscott, home of William Morris, the book was printed in the village of Barnsley in the manner of the great artist-craftsmen of Morris's day on a press that he would have been at once familiar with, and is a perfect presentation in which to capture the very essence of the much loved writings of Rosemary Verey. The extracts are reproduced here with the kind permission of Davina Wynne-Jones, copyright holder and publisher-printer of Gryffon Publications.

CHURCH DECORATIONS

It always falls to my lot to do the church flowers in December. This dates back to the years when we grew chrysanthemums and always

Rosemary Verey in her winter garden, who said, '*A garden in winter is the absolute test of the true gardener. True gardening is as much about the bones of a garden as its planting. If your garden looks good in winter, you belong to a select band capable of bending nature to its will.*'

had plenty to fill the vases. Now the greenhouse space is occupied by scented-leaved pelargoniums and a variety of other tender plants but no chrysanthemums. For the first Sunday in the month I had a lovely time wandering in the garden. Flowers were scarce; a few bedraggled roses, the last of the nerines and some fragrant *Viburnum bodnantense* were the only possibilities so instead I settled for decorative leaves. How satisfying this proved to be; sprays of grey eucalyptus to contrast with apple-green hart's tongue ferns, golden privet and golden lonicera, blending with holly 'Silver Queen' and dark green ivies with variegated periwinkles. There are still plenty of berries about so I chose a selection of white, yellow and red sorbus. I am not adept at flower arranging, but the sheer quality of the foliage and berries was exciting.

NEW YEAR INTO 1980

This New Year's Eve as the clock strikes midnight the eighties start. A quick glance back over the past ten years and country people will remember the great drought, the great frost, the hue and cry raised against hunting and coursing, the increased vogue for visiting historic country houses, their estate and gardens. What perhaps are less obvious to us are the increasingly grave threats to the plant kingdom, with over 25,000 flowering plant species believed to be in danger. A Red Data Book compiled at Kew and published in 1978 by the International Union for Conservation of Nature and Natural Resources gives detailed histories of 250 threatened plants from a wide range of different habitats. One of our resolutions for the next ten years could be to become more positive in promoting conservation of our country surroundings. Leisure for town dwellers will mean extra time spent in the country so the countryside will inevitably get more wear and tear but let us hope it will be associated with an increase in awareness and respect and a decrease in vandalism. For as Moses Cook wrote over 300 years ago, "Those that are wasters and wilful spoilers of trees and plants, without just reason to do so, have seldom prospered in this world."

BIBLIOGRAPHY, SOURCES AND SUGGESTED FURTHER READING

A Christmas Carol: Charles Dickens (1843)

A Cotswold Village: J. Arthur Gibbs, originally published by John Murray (1898) – paperback edition by Nonsuch Publishing (2005)

A Cotswold Year: C. Henry Warren, published by Geoffrey Bles (1936)

A Country Christmas: Johnny Coppin, published by The Windrush Press (1996)

A Countrywoman's Notes: Rosemary Verey, published by Gryffon Publications (1989)

All About Cookery: Mrs Isabella Beeton, (1901)

A Victorian Rector and Nine Old Maids: Michael Boyes, published by Phillimore & Co. Ltd Chichester, West Sussex PO20 2BG (2005)

Collections of John Moore's works – The John Moore Society. Website: philrobbins@yahoo.co.uk

Cotswold Life magazines, published by Archant Life. Website: www.cotswoldlife.co.uk

East Cotswold Church Monthly, December (1968)

EKCO'S of Cowbridge, House and War Factory: Bob Browning, published by Cowbridge Publishing Malmesbury SN16 9LZ (2005)

Fairford and Lechlade Voices: June Lewis-Jones, published by Tempus Publishing (2001)

Family Tree Magazine, published by ABM Publishing Ltd. Website: www.family-tree.co.uk

Folklore of the Cotswolds: June Lewis-Jones, published by Tempus Publishing (2003)

Gloucestershire Countryside magazines (issues dated as given in credits preceding feature)

Gloucestershire Stories: Hope Costley White, published by The British Publishing Company, Gloucester (1949)

Gloucestershire Record Office

Lays and Legends of Gloucestershire: Adin Williams, published by Savory's Steam Press, Cirencester (1879)

Mr and Mrs Charles Dickens Entertain at Home: Stuart Dickens McHugh and Helen Cox, published by Pergamon General Books (1970)

Queen's College Archives, Oxford University

Stroud's Birthplace: Diana Harris and Tracy Spiers (2003) – Enquiries through Stroud Maternity Hospital

Sunday at Home 1905-06, published by The Religious Tract Society

The Jubilee Boy: Richard Martin and Judith Fay, published by the Filkins Press, Cotswold Woollen Weavers, Filkins, Lechlade, Glos (1987)

The Midnight Storytellers – website: www.midnightstorytellers.co.uk

The Secret Diary of Sarah Thomas: June Lewis, published by The Windrush Press (1994)

The Sunlight on the Garden: Elizabeth Speller, published by Granta (2006)

The Witch's Mark: June Lewis, published by Robert Hale (1975)

West Country Christmas Album: Johnny Coppin, produced by Red Sky Records

Wilts and Gloucestershire Standard – website: www.wiltsglosstandard.co.uk

Index of Extracts